A11701 646855

D0131047

COP 1

77 REF. SERV.

A11701 646855

M. I. Hümmel

HUMMEL

HUMMEL

the complete
collector's guide
and illustrated
reference

design by John Peace

illustration by Robert Frost

HUMMEL

the complete collector's guide and illustrated reference

**BY
ERIC EHRMANN**

photography by
SEYMOUR LINDEN

special contributor
ROBERT L. MILLER

special consultant
LOUISE SCHAUB WITT

**1976
PORTFOLIO PRESS CORPORATION**
Huntington, New York 11743

FIRST EDITION ● SECOND PRINTING

*Copyright © 1976 Portfolio Press Corporation. All rights reserved.
Published in New York, New York, and simultaneously in
Toronto, Canada, and in London, England. Printed in the
United States of America.*

*Portions of the text of this work were first published
in* Acquire *magazine under the titles "The Facts About Hummel
Collecting," and "The Hummel History: Part II," both copyright ©
1975 Acquire Publishing Co., Inc.*
Library of Congress Cataloging in Publication Data.

Let's ramble down a happy path
To a joyful and placid land.
Where childrens' faces and angels' graces
Raise the spirit of man.

We'll smile and laugh
Along the path.
We'll take time for reflection.

A moment seized from daily life.
A worthwhile recollection.

E.W.E.

TABLE OF CONTENTS

INTRODUCTION

The history of Hummel is extraordinary. In less than half a century, the popularity of these innocently delightful *kinder* has risen to include millions of collectors in almost every nation on earth. Heads of state, dignitaries, and celebrities are among the millions. But in spite of this widespread appeal of Hummel figurines, there has never been a book that showcased the entire collection or answered the questions most often raised by astute collectors. Here, at long last, is what Hummel figurine collectors have been clamoring for.

The book begins with a definitive biography of Berta Hummel, who, as Sister Maria Innocentia Hummel, created the art that is the basis for the most sought-after figurines in the world. Sister Maria Innocentia's artistic vision relied heavily upon her own childhood in the tranquility of a remote Bavarian village in her native Germany. Her tragic illness and death in a war-torn land underline a universal need to occasionally retire from the hard realities of everyday life and return for a little while to the happier, less complex, turn-of-the-century themes that Sister Maria Innocentia recorded. This is the essence and spirit that radiates from every "M.I. Hummel" figurine.

The entire Hummel figurine collection is included in the gallery section of this book. There is also an exclusive reproduction of America's—if not the world's—most prolific collection of Hummel figurine rarities. Other chapters discuss the marking system used on all figurines, how they are made, and by whom.

In preparing this book, the author traveled thousands of miles over many months conducting interviews in German and English. In Germany alone, there were more than 200 interviews, ranging from members of the Hummel family and Sister Maria Innocentia's convent, to now-retired craftsmen who once worked on the figurines that bear her images. In the United States, countless collectors gave valuable information for the project, especially about rare and unique pieces. The result of all this effort is now in your hands. Enjoy it!

CHAPTER
I: BERTA'S CHILDHOOD

Illustration of a young girl by
Sister Maria Innocentia Hummel.

Deep in Lower Bavaria where the rolling farmland gives way to the foothills of the Alps, a legend exists about the *Schauerfreitag,* the Friday-born child. According to this bit of ancient folklore, those born on Friday are often gifted with vivid imaginations. They rarely occupy themselves with day-to-day chores. They are different. Berta Hummel was a Friday-born child.

On a cold, drizzly spring day in 1975 in the Bavarian village of Massing an der Rott Berta Hummel's mother, Viktoria, proudly reminisced about her daughter's early childhood in those distant years prior to World War I. "By the time Berta was three, we knew she was a real *Schauerfreitag.* She would often sit by the light of a window with a pencil in her hand, daydreaming and scribbling." The mother, then on the eve of her ninetieth birthday, sat erect and without a trace of infirmity, her dark eyes twinkling behind wire-rim glasses. The walls were covered with paintings and the family albums bulged with sketches, small drawings, and photographs of the artistic Berta.

In the spacious hallways of the house are carefully arranged cases containing the charming children-dominated figurines that were created from the famous drawings done by Berta in her artistic prime, when she served as the Franciscan nun, Sister Maria Innocentia Hummel.

Berta was born on May 21, 1909, the third daughter of Adolf and Viktoria Hummel. Like all of her brothers and sisters, Berta was born in the three-story stuccoed concrete building that has housed both family and business through four generations. The scalloped Italian facade and the simple sign, "J. Hummel," remain just as they appeared in the years of Berta's childhood. Today, ready-to-wear clothing has replaced dry goods as the essential part of the family's store.

Berta Hummel's mother recalled vividly the era more than sixty years ago when her daughter was born. Her husband ran the family business, dealing with farmers who came to the tiny hamlet for each week's open market. "As a youth, Adolf always wanted to become an artist," said Viktoria Hummel, "but since he was an only son, it was his duty to carry on in his father's footsteps. He spent a great deal of his spare time making woodcarvings and woodcuts, but it was only a hobby."

Berta turned five in 1914, on the eve of the First World War. At that time life in Massing, like that of most rural Bavarian towns, revolved around a strong family alliance and the Roman Catholic church. The Hummel household was no different. Adolf Hummel's modest success in business enabled Viktoria to hire a live in cook-housekeeper to ease the burden of raising the children, but it did not keep seven-year-old Katje and six-year-old Vicki from performing such daily chores as sweeping, beating rugs, washing windows, or gardening. Berta, as her mother recalled, was quite different.

"If she wasn't using wastepaper from the store downstairs to make her drawings, she would be looking for old scraps of cloth to make dolls clothes. Often Lisa, our cook, would help her sew little costumes for the dolls. They were simple, but very colorful. When they finished Berta would go out into the garden or into the kitchen or wherever her two older sisters happened to be busy and put on a little show with the dolls to entertain them." Berta was living up to the nickname her mother had given her, *Das Hummele* the German word for bumblebee, buzzing from one idea to another. On later occasions, Berta would employ her brother Ady, dressing him in anything from her mother's shawl to a bedsheet to fabricate a makeshift knight's costume or some other outfit that fit one of the various heroes of German folklore, in order to perform spontaneous pantomimes after dinner in front of the family.

These *Märchen* (folk tales) served to pass on the local folklore in an imaginative manner during the days when creative kindergartens and television were part of the distant and unknown future. "The little shows always made my father happy," Berta's brother Adolf remembered, "and he didn't seem to mind that Berta was different from the rest of us when it came to responsibilities around the house. Mind you, she was no favorite, but *Vati* (father) always wanted someone in the family to become an artist, so he let her do as she pleased."

War broke out on July 23, 1914, and within a few months Adolf Hummel was conscripted into the Kaiser's army. Viktoria Hummel then had to preside over the family business and raise the children, who with the birth of Franz on September 15, 1914, numbered six. With the war came food shortages, and the Hummel family, having a better-than-average position in the town of Massing, opened its doors to those neighbors and townfolk who were less fortunate. The diversity of Berta's playmates rapidly increased from a sphere that consisted of her brothers and sisters to a group of children she had previously seen only at Sunday church or Saturday market. Often Frau Hummel would invite these children for Sunday dinner, and give them small gifts they could not afford to buy at the dry-goods store.

"*Mutti* (mother) would give the little girls hair ribbons or kerchiefs and the boys would get pocket combs or new collars to wear with their Sunday shirts to church," Adolf reminisced. "And always afterward, Berta would put on a little show. Not only were these playmates her friends, but her best audience as well."

One of her most famous plays, according to her mother, was done at the age of six—her interpretation of the Grimm fairy tale *Hansel and Gretel*. "Later in her life, Berta's sketches of Hansel and Gretel were made into figurines," Frau Hummel said. "She liked to perform outdoors best, and every Sunday during those springs and summers our backyard was so crowded that Berta began charging admission!"

Of course this admission was not money, it was anything the youngsters could find in the way of clothing or props to keep Berta Hummel's Sunday performances going and producing new shows. And the humble star of the show was always the young, buzzing little *Hummele*. Even the mothers of the children began coming to the Hummel theatre.

In 1917, when she was eight years old, Berta Hummel gave a performance of the *Märchen, Die Hexe* (the sorcerer), but there was little magic a young girl could brew to change the tide of sadness that crept in around her townspeople as the news from the front lines began to indicate that her nation was losing a very costly and embittered war. "Berta always read the letters her father sent us from his unit," Frau Hummel said. "Sometimes he would begin writing and have to stop in the middle of his letter because of the shelling. After reading mail like this, Berta would try to do things to make him happy. She made colorful postcards and illustrated the borders of the letters we sent. Her father always encouraged her to continue with her art, and it was sad for Berta that he could not be at home during these years to guide her."

Shortly after her sixth birthday, Berta entered school. The very strict educational traditions of Prussian-dominated imperial Germany that were developed during the era of Bismarck had filtered down into Bavaria as well, with the exception that the church, rather than the state administered many of the local small-town schools. The *Volksschule* (people's school) in Massing, run by the Sisters of Notre Dame, was such a school. Similar in curricula to the old schoolhouses of American frontier days, it had only two levels, with children between the ages of six and fifteen sitting in the same class, having to listen to their classmates recite daily lessons from books resembling *McGuffey's Eclectic Reader*.

"Berta," her mother said, "spent more time drawing than paying attention to what was going on in class." But the sisters who ran the *Volksschule* in Massing were blessed with the gift of patience, for they knew that their students, coming from poor or modest families, were like the large majority of the young people in Germany who had no chance of advancing to the prestigious *Gymnasium* (college prep school) that would enable them to pursue a university education. They were destined to either return to their family farms or businesses, or possibly to learn a trade.

According to her mother, Berta suffered from the absence of her father during these war years. Her lack of discipline was often disguised by her budding talent and amiable disposition, but when the school sisters of Massing tried to indoctrinate her to the disciplined ways of school life, she had ways of retaliating. She would always try to be the center of attraction in the classroom, just as she had been at home, passing around her drawings or making witty comments that had nothing at all to do with the lessons. When her name was put on the blackboard to stay after classes for insubordination she would erase it during a recess. When the school sisters tried to counsel her, she became coy and uncommunicative.

Frau Hummel was called to the school for a conference regarding Berta's attitude and general lack of bearing. "The sisters asked us to be vigilant at home and even to use force in disciplining Berta," Viktoria Hummel said. "But she was not the same at home as she was at school. How could Adolf be violent with her after going through a war like that?"

After the First World War, the free state of Bavaria was suffering from defeat and chaos like the rest of Germany. Skyrocketing inflation took hold of the economy after King Ludwig III, the constitutional monarch, was deposed by a socialist-communist coup in Munich on the night of November 7, 1918, four days prior to the signing of the Armistice. The socialist-communist coalition leader, Eisner, threatened the farmers with collectivization of their lands, and the businesses and factories with expropriation until his assassination on February 21, 1919. In reaction, communist workers descended upon Munich and the city was besieged with rioting and looting in the streets. The *Landtag* (state house of representatives) was closed on August 12, 1919, and the Bavarian Constitution was absolved. It was under this backdrop of uncertainty that Adolf Hummel tried to reconstruct his business and his role as father after returning from the costly war.

Drawing by Sister M. I. Hummel that is the basis for figurine model HUM 21 "Heavenly Angel."

When Frau Hummel made her visit to the *Volksschule* in Massing to discuss the classroom behavior and work habits of Berta, she asked the sisters to be understanding in light of the times and to discontinue their idea of imposing "hickory stick" punishment on her daughter. "We were lucky," she remembered, "because there was one school sister, Sister Theresa, who recognized Berta's talents as a budding artist and praised her in front of the others who wanted to discipline her." Under the watchful eye of Sister Theresa, Berta Hummel was promoted to the fourth or final form of the Massing *Volksschule.* With a good recommendation from Sister Theresa, Berta was admitted to the *Institut der Englischen Fräulein,* (Institute of English Sisters) a prestigious boarding school at Simbach, some twenty miles east of Massing on the Inn River.

The Institute, which stands on a bluff high above the town, is known to local townspeople as *Marienhohe.* Today, the great view from *Marienhohe* across the Inn River, which forms Germany's natural boundary with Austria, is partially blocked by new housing developments, apartment buildings, and small factories. But in 1921, when Berta Hummel matriculated at the school, there was nothing to obstruct the imagination of a young *Schauerfreitag* as she rambled in the lush meadows, looking for wild flowers to brighten her dormitory room during her first days away from home.

If life at Simbach was going to be rewarding for Berta Hummel, she would have to crack the books as well as sketch or go exploring in the fields. As a result of her inattentiveness to the traditional subjects taught at the *Volksschule* in Massing, she was actually one year older than the rest of her classmates. Still, her art pulled her through Simbach. Tutoring succeeded in drawing Berta equal with her classmates and she was

allowed to skip the remainder of her first year a few months after she entered the school, resuming a normal cycle of academic progress.

The Institute had an art department and for the first time Berta Hummel found herself in an academic atmosphere which was able to give direction to the graphic talent she acquired almost instinctively as a young child. During her Simbach years she became a teen-ager. Under the direction of excellent teachers, her artistic energies were channeled into projects which benefited the entire school. She designed scenery and costumes for the school plays, much in the same way she had in her backyard theatre at home in Massing; but instead of the audience being a handful of local children, it was several hundred students, faculty members, and parents in the auditorium of the institution.

The Simbach years were also the years in which Berta Hummel first became interested in watercolors, using them in her earliest attempts at painting landscapes. Her art class would frequently go on nature walks across the border into Austria, or take weekend tours into the Upper Bavarian Alps. She would also spend summers at the home of her great aunt in the alpine town of Berchtesgaden. "Berta would sketch and paint the mountain scenery for hours," her mother reminisced. "Both her father and I began to sense a change that first summer after she entered Simbach. She was doing much more than sketches of her classmates and the little fantasies that used to take place around the house. The progress made her father very proud."

By her fourth year at Simbach, 1925, Berta had branched out into other areas of self-expression. She commenced working with terra cotta clay, sculpting animals and faces. She also began using her imagination to create pen and ink illustrations of the famous German fairy tale characters that she had discovered back home in Massing at an earlier age and which had served as the subject matter of her backyard theatre plays. These included *Hansel and Gretel* from the Brothers Grimm collection and Weber's *Dreizehn Linden* (Thirteen Tales).

Her illustrations of the Weber tales, which draw their roots from the epic folklore surrounding the Germanic gods, rest today in the archives of the Institute at Simbach. These first attempts of a sixteen-year-old girl, who as a daydreaming child had earned the nickname *Schauerfreitag,* are in the same tradition of the fairy tale characters and feelings she illuminated. A short decade later, her sketches as Sister Maria Innocentia Hummel would be translated into ceramics by W. Goebel as "M.I. Hummel" figurines.

Life at Simbach had been demanding for Berta Hummel, but at the same time it proved to be the right atmosphere for her adolescent years. There were a daily wake-ups at five a.m. followed by mandatory morning Mass. Also part of the curriculum were required courses in catechism and the history of the Catholic church. "Berta began learning politeness and how to respect others, as well as the lyceum subjects," her mother recalled. "She began coming home with religious anecdotes and biblical tales instead of the fairy tales that amused her so much when she was home." The spartan religious environment had become an important part of her life, weaving itself into the fibre of her existence to establish a fabric of maturity and strength.

At the Massing *Volksschule,* Sister Theresa had gone to bat for her in front of a faculty irritated by her antics. Now at Simbach there was Sister Stephania, the art professor, who took Berta under her wing, giving guidance and insight to a talented pupil who preferred to communicate with the silence of a sketch instead of the sound of words. "Berta would bring her work home when she came for a weekend or a holiday," her mother remembered. "She was painting still lifes, nature scenes, and of course continuing her little sketches on postcards. My husband began noticing refinement in her style, a self-confidence that let him know Berta really wanted to fulfill his ambition by becoming the family artist."

During her final year at Simbach, Berta began assisting Sister Stephania in the teaching of her elementary art class. She was cooperating with them and helping her sister students as well. Sister Stephania encouraged Berta to continue her art education after graduating from Simbach, with the hope that the *Hummele* would become an art teacher like herself. She counseled Adolf and Viktoria Hummel about their daughter's future, emphasizing the difficulty of becoming a recognized artist during the depressed decade that followed World War I.

Sister Stephania suggested to Adolf and Viktoria Hummel that their daughter continue her education by taking the curriculum for art teachers at the Academy of Applied Arts in Munich. She wrote an excellent recommendation on behalf of her favorite pupil. "Berta would have plenty of time to live the life of a young artist," her mother said, "but she would also be gaining the security of having a profession. Education was not cheap in those days either, especially considering the terrible inflation. We had put Katje and Vicki through girls' school at Simbach and Adolf was attending the boys' school there at the same time as Berta. Centa and Franzl would soon be ready for Simbach, too. The extra money we needed to send Berta to Munich was a sacrifice for the whole family, but it was well worth the joy it gave my husband when he read her letters and saw the illustrations and paintings she brought home over the holidays."

The postwar inflation had indeed hit Massing just as hard as it had Berlin or Munich or Dresden, the loosely knit economies of the small rural towns finding no shelter from the constant erosion of the value of the German currency. In the family library of the

Hummel home in Massing, a chart of the incredible decline in worth of the old German *Reichsmark* is displayed to invited visitors as a grim reminder of those lean days. "In 1924 it took three million of those old *Reichsmarks* to buy one kilo (2¼ lbs.) of black bread," Berta's brother Adolf recalled. "My mother used to ask me to fill a washtub with money when she wanted to go to the bakery. When we wanted to buy pastries or chocolate for Sundays or holidays I had to fill two."

Herr Hummel was a wise businessman and held a privileged place in the Massing infrastructure, earning an income which, even in those hard times, was able to send his children to a private boarding school. His kind heart saw him extending credit to many of his customers, often taking large quantities of farm products in barter or cattle or horses he did not need as payment for past-due accounts. Sometimes, when he had taken in an overabundance of perishables, Frau Hummel would run the egg and vegetable stand on market days just to sell off everything her husband had taken in on trade. "Many times," she recalled, "I remember giving food away. The war had done something to my husband's soul. His heart was with the family, but not with the business. This is why he was so proud that Berta could experience a different kind of life by studying in Munich."

CHAPTER 2: THE MUNICH YEARS

In the fall of 1927, Adolf Hummel took a few days off from his business to accompany his daughter Berta to Munich, making the fifty-mile journey by train. "When he came back he felt just like a schoolboy," Centa Hummel, Berta's youngest sister, said. "He looked renewed, mainly because Berta was following his own childhood ambition."

Centa Hummel closely resembles her late sister. Living in the city of Passau, where the rivers Inn and Donau converge at the Austrian border to form the greater Danube, she teaches applied gymnastics at a private girls' school. In her home hang several Hummel paintings and icons, as well as an oil portrait of her done by her sister, all of which were done after Berta entered the Franciscan Convent at Seissen.

"When Berta first arrived in Munich, she and our father went around looking for a student room that would meet his specifications," Centa said. "They found a pension near the Convent and Church of Saint Ann. That's where she spent her first few months. She would write home that she was very lonely and that the other students who rented rooms at the pension were not too friendly. It was her first experience away from the religious school dormitory, and the life of a big-city student seemed quite foreign to her. Shortly afterward, she moved into a religious dormitory run by the order of the Holy Family in the Blumenstrasse, which offered an environment very much like that of Simbach. Everyone was very serious and the rules were very strict. "When I first went to Munich to study," said Centa, "I followed Berta's example and roomed there. But for me there was too much discipline, so I moved into a small apartment with a school friend."

During the late 1920s, the *Akademie für Angewandte Kunst* was one of the major innovational centers of design and applied arts in Germany. It trained students who wished to become art teachers and those who desired to apply their skills practically in industry or on their own. Specific paths of study were offered in textile weaving and design, book printing and binding, ceramics, sculpture, graphic design, glass blowing, architecture, and in the manufacture and cutting of crystal.

The Academy was directed by Professor Carlo Sattler, an architect and ceramic artist. Sattler was a friend of the American banker James Loeb, a patron of the arts and universities in his ancestral home of Munich as well as in the United States. Along with several of his professors, Sattler was a member of the *Deutsche Werkbund*—a professional association of teachers, artists, designers, and architects who had a great influence on the applied arts and on their institutions of learning. The influence of the *Werkbund* filtered down to the students at the academy, where ripe young minds welcomed fresh ideas with the hope of painting a brighter picture of the world than the sad drudgery of a nation trying to struggle to its feet after losing a war.

"*Werkbund* was the most important movement in art and design that came out of southern Germany, starting about 1910," according to Otto Hufnagel, a former classmate of Berta Hummel at the Munich Academy. "It followed the *Jugendstil* period, coming into public and critical attention at least ten years before the rival *Bauhaus*

The Munich Academy of Applied Arts at Richard Wagnerstrasse 10, circa 1931. The building is now the Paleontological Institute of Munich University.

movement began in the northcentral German city of Weimar. Munich, being a predominantly Catholic city, was the logical center for such a movement since religious art and church design had given the city its particular ambience. But there were also groups of *Werkbund* artists, designers, and students in Vienna and Zurich."

The main thrust of the *Werkbund* movement was an attempt to build upon the great artistic traditions of the Baroque and Florentine periods, incorporating these styles into contemporary design concepts. A few years after the end of the First World War, the *Bauhaus* school of design—in direct opposition to the curved, flowing lines of *Werkbund*—began receiving critical attention. "*Werkbund* was a spirit," Hufnagel, who today is the director of the Bavarian State School for Ceramics in Landshut, added. "*Bauhaus* was straight sharp lines, very Protestant in its following, and very much a symbol of the north. We were the south."

Later in her life, Berta Hummel painted icons, murals, and religious frescoes using Baroque and Florentine styles modernized through her exposure to the *Werkbund* movement at the Munich Academy. "Had Berta Hummel studied in Berlin," Hufnagel continued, "she would have had an entirely different experience."

Berta attended the *Berufsfachschule*, a special section of the Academy that offered a curriculum to prospective teachers of general art in elementary and high schools. Here she had the opportunity to work in a secular environment for the first time, and expanded her talents into the areas of rug weaving, clothes design, and sculpture. She studied drawing with Professor Max Dasio, well known for his illustrations in children's books and his woodcuts of German folklore characters. Seizing the opportunity to form, refine, and perhaps influence an emerging talent, Professor Dasio quickly invited Berta Hummel into his inner circle. Eventually, she became Dasio's prize pupil, the student-teacher rapport being so great that he urged her to take a position as his teaching assistant upon her graduation from the Academy.

"Dasio was definitely her most important influence at the Academy," Otto Hufnagel remembered. "Some students arrive at a new school and talk about their past exploits; but Berta Hummel wasn't that way. She made a quick impression on fellow students and professors with her excellent sketching technique. She was quiet, very pretty, and in my opinion a bit withdrawn from the social life that went along with school. Of course, this may have been due to her small-town background and the years she spent away from home in strict religious schools; but at the same time she was clever, possessing a fantastic humor and a quick wit that would pop up when you least expected it. Dasio was a quick-witted person, too, and it was this match of wits that saw them get along so well."

The square, arcaded hallways of the four-story building, skylit by translucent glass roof tiles, were perfect places for Berta Hummel to find quick sketching subjects for Professor Dasio's class. Between classes, students would linger along the balustrades of the arcades, their faces illuminated by pure daylight. Here they kept canvases, smocks, and paints in individual lockers. Often a couple of students would be leaning leisurely against the Corinthian-pillared arcades having a quick conversation, unknowingly becoming the subject of a Berta Hummel sketch. By the time the next class started she would have either presented the sketch to the students or taken it to Professor Dasio for his approval and praise. Today, the battleship gray and white stucco facade of the art school still stands at Richard Wagnerstrasse 10, but the school moved to the Akademiestrasse after the Second World War. The old building now serves as the Paleontological Institute of Munich University.

Sister M. I. Hummel's drawing of "Little Fiddler,"
which is the basis for the HUM 2 figurine.

The old Academy was less than a five-minute walk from the *Alte Pinakothek*, the most famous art museum in Bavaria, where Berta Hummel, along with her fellow students in the color and composition class of Professor Richard Klein, would go to study the works of Albrecht Durer, Rubens, Van Dyck, El Greco, and Murillo. Her visits to this museum brought her close to the masters for the first time. The exposure also served to broaden her scope of art beyond the borders of Germany. "She talked of wanting to go to Florence or Venice to study and paint," her mother remembered.

Berta Hummel's art education was, of course, entirely Bavarian. But the ideas that she picked up during her frequent research visits to the Munich museums, her reading of the art text and biographical commentary on the lives of Giotto, Michelangelo, and the

other masters, combined with the stimulus of the *Werkbund* movement, eventually found their way into her work. Some of it can be seen in the churches in which Sister Innocentia Hummel was commissioned to paint or sculpt a particular religious figure. Her *"Teilbild der Pieta"* ("Mural of Piety") in Tuttlingen, the "Infant of Krumbad" in Krumbad, and the mural at the church of Saint Stephen in Massing of Brother Conrad distributing bread to the poor, are three examples of this art.

Berta Hummel's desire to travel to the great art centers of Europe and her newly focused attention on the old masters came as a shock to both her and her family. The amount of cultural sophistication she had absorbed during her first two years in Munich

completely overshadowed the education and values instilled by her parents and her convent schooling.

She was still, however, very much a product of Catholic Bavaria, of quiet, small-town life that went on with the pace of the horse and buggy or river barge that continued to symbolize transportation in her native area. The attachment to her family was deep, as was the commitment to please her father within the framework of his modest understanding of art. She was familiar with the concepts of sacrifice and self-denial, for they had been articulated since her preschool days, from the *Volksschule* at Massing to the institute in Simbach. These concepts continued to linger quietly but heavily at her side, comprising the weight of the two most important institutions in her life: church and family. Living as a *Heimchen* (boarding student) at the Holy Family residence reminded the happy buzzing bee that after she finished working and gathering knowledge at the Academy, her fate would see her hovering close to home. Thus she was not destined to venture far; the field trips with the watercolor class of Professor Else Brauneis to the Austrian city of Salzburg and the Upper Bavarian resort towns of Garmisch and Partenkirchen were the greatest distances she was to stray.

As in Simbach, the atmosphere of the Holy Family residence was conducted with the strictness of a convent, for it was administered by sisters. Silence was the rule in the hallways, but Berta Hummel always scuffed her heels. Beds were to be made without a wrinkle, but Berta's was always messy. Floors were to be swept clean each morning before breakfast, wardrobes dusted, and sundries kept in order; but Berta Hummel, being the art student in the dormitory, proudly hung her paintings on the walls in violation of the rules, and her pencils, brushes, and paints strewn everywhere across her room. Once again she was the exception to the rules, but once again her talent gained her special friendship and respect. This time it was two young Franciscan Sisters who were staying at the Holy Family residence while studying art at the Akademie. Sister Laura and Sister Kostka were sympathetic toward their new friend and always came to her aid.

Berta's imagination and penchant for doing the things that made her life as a *Heimchen* just a little bit more frivolous managed to overshadow the disciplinary atmosphere of the residence. Instead of rebelling against her superiors, she outwitted them, using her talent and wit to win the sympathy of her sister students when a particular Hummel prank would come to the attention of the Holy Family hierarchy. Male visitors were strictly forbidden, and, as a general rule, relatives and parents were not permitted inside the residence unless approved in advance by the Mother Superior.

One February, Berta Hummel was bemused by the devil-may-care spirit of *Fasching* (Carnival or Mardi Gras) that reigns each year prior to Ash Wednesday. She decided to bend the rules. "She told her Mother Superior that she had invited special visitors to the Holy Family *Fasching* party," Frau Hummel recalled. "But she kept the identity of these visitors a secret for weeks. The Mother Superior thought Berta was going to bring male guests for the celebration."

Compared with what would be going on elsewhere around town, the Holy Family *Fasching* party would be a tame affair. The Bavarian capital took its *Fasching* very seriously, with no holds barred, much like Mardi Gras in New Orleans or Carnival in Rio de Janeiro. The one concession that the superiors made to the *Heimchen* was that the affair could be a masked ball—and that gave Berta Hummel all the ammunition she needed. Resident students would be showing up as princes and paupers, soldiers and clowns, and the big worry of the Mother Superior would be how to determine the sex of the guests behind the Hummel-designed masks and costumes. Berta had told the Mother Superior that her guests would be ringing the doorbell around half past eight on carnival night, and once the word got around everyone at the residence was waiting with excitement for the next Hummel coup.

With the sound of the chime, the students all ran down to the parlor to greet the surprise guests with a deeply concerned Mother Superior not far behind. But to their surprise, Berta Hummel had pulled yet another trick out of her seemingly bottomless bag. Standing in the parlor of the Holy Family residence hall were fully clothed papier-mâché models of all her professors: Dasio, Klein, and Brauneis. The Mother Superior was greatly relieved, to say the least.

But playing the role of court jester in a stringent, religious dormitory environment was only one of the sides of Berta Hummel. During this time, her friendship with the two Franciscan Sisters, Sister Laura and Sister Kostka, strengthened, and with it an interest in religious life that hinted her future direction to those around her. "The closer she came to the two sisters," Otto Hufnagel recalled, "the more it became certain that Berta Hummel would eventually join their convent. This irked Dasio very much because she was his prodigy. He wanted her to continue on as his assistant after taking her degree."

Her second year in Munich saw her friendship with the two Franciscan Sisters continue. Her father had just begun to enjoy the happy life he had led before the war. "It had taken him ten years to recover from the war, the hard times, and his shrapnel wounds," said Centa Hummel. "Now, with Vicki's death he became more distant again, and this affected Berta, who was of course a very gentle and emotional person. She was strong in spirit, but she was the kind of person who had so much energy that she would run herself down until her whole body would weaken and she would need to spend weeks on end in bed fighting off the flu. Her reaction to the tragedy was to work harder because she wanted to please her father and become a success. The increased interest in religious life seemed to be her way of giving thanks for all she had. It seemed to represent one part of her personality, and if it was the dominating one she kept it to herself."

The year 1929 gave twenty-year-old Berta Hummel good reason for leaning toward a religious life. Munich, capital of Bavaria and the largest city in southern Germany, had become a haven for the dissatisfied and unemployed; and the magnet that had drawn them was Adolf Hitler's National Socialist German Workers' Party. The marching and singing of the Brownshirts was a common sight during the daytime, and at night the beer halls would fill with the Nazi sympathizers who came to hear Party speakers, drink strong beer, and talk of *Putsch*. At the Academy, students sympathetic to Hitler's cause formed propagandistic youth groups to propagate their ideas and gain new followers among the students of the applied arts.

Upon graduation, the Party would find them jobs, funneling them into critical areas of German culture: advertising, architecture, and graphic design. Waiting in the wings, they would continue their Party activity, organizing for the inevitable political victory that would earn them good positions with the propaganda ministry of Josef Goebbels. Berta Hummel was hardly the kind of individual who wished to tie her educational experience to the success of the Third Reich.

Berta Hummel's bond of friendship with the two Franciscan Sisters brought about changes in her life. "The sisters were regarded as outsiders by most of the students," Otto

A self portrait done by Sister Maria Innocentia Hummel.

Hufnagel said. "They were very quiet and didn't communicate with anyone except their professors and Berta. They would go to class, eat lunch, and disappear." More and more Berta Hummel followed their example.

Berta would pray each morning at the *Frauenkirche* (The Church of Our Lady) before arriving at school. The church, whose twin onion-shaped domes break the skyline across the flat plain of Munich, was on her daily route from Holy Family residence hall to the Academy making it very convenient. The *Frauenkirche* is a majestic structure, ranking as one of the world's outstanding examples of pure Gothic style. Twenty-two octagonal pillars vault the sanctuary roof to a height of one hundred feet, giving a visitor the illusion that all the windows in the church are blocked by its buttresses. Bavarian legend has it that when the devil inspected the church and found no windows, he stamped his foot in delight. In correspondence with this legend, there is a special footprint of the "devil's step" in the vestibule that leads to the cathedral.

Berta Hummel received self-confidence from her religion, for it was the most consistent and dominating theme that ran through her life. The huge *Frauenkirche* in Munich was as much a world away from the small parish church of Saint Stephen in Massing, as the tiny two-level *Volksschule* was from the prestigious Academy. At the age of twenty-two, in 1931, she had come a long way—further than the opportunities of a small-town Bavarian girl would generally suggest. Her artwork at the Academy had given her considerable notoriety among her fellow students, and she held the highest grade point average in her class. As a result, the pressure upon her to make a solid decision about her future was mounting.

On one hand, Professors Max Dasio and Else Brauneis were trying to convince her to continue on at the Academy, both offering to employ her as a graduate teaching assistant. It would have meant a successful, comfortable existence: a secure job, an income, and a leisurely artist's life that revolved around Schwabing, Munich's art colony.

But would this lifestyle remain such a relaxed and fun-filled existence within the changing political climate? There was already a movement on to oust Academy director Carlo Sattler, one of the most important figures in the *Werkbund*, from his position because he was married to a woman with Jewish parentage. Adjusting to this new order would mean a forced break with her entire religious upbringing and education, and a yielding to the chaos and uncertainty of the moment. On the other hand, there was the quiet but persevering example of the two Franciscan Sisters, Laura and Kostka. Seeking sanctuary behind the walls of a convent would permit Berta Hummel to continue her art, to teach, and to live a life that knew a duty only to eternal time instead of the Party, the Reich, or the Führer.

On March 15, 1931, Berta Hummel graduated from the *Akademie für Angewandte Kunst* in Munich, first in her class. It was a proud day for the entire Hummel family—all of whom went to Munich for the occasion—and especially for her father Adolf, who was seeing his daughter succeed in a métier that to him had been but a fleeting dream. What few knew on that graduation day was that Berta Hummel had already decided upon her destiny. It was a decision made with silence and delicacy, an act that would chafe the feelings of those who held the notion that she would make a much greater contribution to her chosen field in the secular life.

"My parents were not surprised at Berta's decision," Centa Hummel recalled, "for Sisters Laura and Kostka had been to our home in Massing. They knew that Berta was very close to the two Franciscan Sisters and that she was at an important crossroad in her life. But she did keep the actual decision a secret for a period of time. We didn't find out until shortly after her graduation."

Though her parents were not outwardly surprised, Herr Hummel was concerned with his daughter's ability to meet the strenuous demands of religious life. He recalled the disciplinary problems she had incurred at the Massing *Volksschule*, at Simbach, and even at Holy Family. Would Berta Hummel be able to live up to the duties and rules of a convent, he asked his wife. His daughter's decision was the end product of the homelife which he and his wife had supervised, combined with the parochial boarding school education that Herr Hummel himself wished Berta to receive. Berta's Munich years fulfilled her desire to taste the world of art within the secure framework of her religious upbringing. The talent which she refined during her stay there would soon make her name known around the world.

At the Academy in Munich there were sad parting smiles. Berta had made a visit to the home of Professor Else Brauneis to inform her of the decision shortly after graduation. Professor Brauneis was not taken aback by Berta's decision and commenced a lengthy correspondence with her after she entered the convent. But Professor Max Dasio was less enamored with Berta's choice. "She was his cherished pupil," Otto Hufnagel said, "and it was only natural that he felt a degree of disappointment upon finding out. Wouldn't any professor, especially one who was her mentor?" As a going away present, Berta Hummel gave Max Dasio the woodcut of a caricature she had drawn of him. Upon receipt of the gift he looked it over, commenting: "That little rogue of a Hummel could have pulled the drawer out a bit farther." His reference to the "drawer" being his lower lip, which was known to protrude during moments of anger or frustration.

"Dasio finally resigned himself to the fact that Berta had chosen the convent," Centa Hummel said. "He was basically a man who had the philosophy 'everyone does what they will.' " Berta Hummel did exactly that. During the month and a half that passed between her graduation and her prearranged entrance date at the Franciscan Convent at Siessen, she bought new clothing, visited family and acquaintances, and lived a life that hardly reflected her decision to sacrifice all the worldly things she knew and enjoyed. At home in Massing, she spent days quietly sketching, reminiscing, and puttering around the rock garden she had planted when she was younger. But, as Frau Hummel recalled, there was a great deal of emotion upon seeing her off for the journey to Siessen. "We knew she would be coming back to visit," Frau Hummel said, "but we were all concerned with how life at the convent would change her. To us, she would always be Berta."

On April 22, 1931, Berta Hummel entered the convent. The surrounding foothills of the Swabian Alps, greening with spring, were already a familiar sight to her, for she had visited the grounds with Sisters Laura and Kostka a few weeks earlier for a confidential interview. The two sisters had been, of course, an obvious influence on Berta in making her decision to join the Franciscans rather than another Catholic order. Unlike other orders, the Franciscans regard all sisters as equals. There are no choir sisters or lay sisters, no distinctions made between those who have college educations and those who do not. This concept was in keeping with Berta Hummel's humble way of life.

The history of the religious community of Siessen can be traced to the time of the Middle Ages. The name itself, Siessen, means meadowland or pasture, and it was on this kind of terrain outside the town of Saulgau in the old kingdom of Württemberg that in the 13th century a Dominican settlement was formed. During the next six centuries, because of various holy wars, the convent was forced to disband on several occasions. In 1860, twelve years after the confederation of German states was created, the Franciscan Order established a convent around the old nucleus of buildings, creating a teachers' seminary. Later, in 1924, they began devoting themselves to the care of the sick. Their embroidery and lacework also gained them wide renown.

Berta Hummel began teaching art at the teachers' school while a postulant. She also worked with children, traveling by train to several of the sixty-five institutions administered by the Siessen Convent. For a posutlant, her schedule was demanding, but she met it. No longer was she the discipline problem that trademarked her previous encounters with religious education. She was taking her work very seriously and her religion as well. On August 22, 1933, she was given her habit of the Sisters of The Third Order of Saint Francis. As the presiding Bishop cut the symbolic lock of hair from her head, he bestowed upon her a new name: Sister Maria Innocentia.

For someone who had so often been preoccupied with the innocence and simplicity of childhood, the name was appropriate. Innocence had clearly been the main theme running through her life, and when admiring the faces of each "M.I. Hummel" figurine the feeling is always present. "The figurines offer the collector something to look back upon," Otto Hufnagel said. "Childhood is one main feeling that radiates. Innocence is another. The romance of youthful nostalgia is everywhere about them, for that was Berta Hummel's style."

CHAPTER
3: SISTER MARIA INNOCENTIA

The lush meadows of the Swabian Highland, carved and scalloped by the Alpine glaciers long ago, gave Sister Maria Innocentia Hummel a classic landscape view from her studio high atop the Motherhouse of the Siessen Convent. Today, Sister Maria Innocentia's studio stands as a small museum, filled with the sketches, tapestries, and vestments that were part of her contribution to religious and secular art as a member of the Franciscan Order.

Out the windows, a patchwork of lush green grazing land and golden windblown wheat fields offered her a timeless picture of nature, a picture that had been in the back of her mind since the early days of her Lower Bavarian childhoold. Between 1931 and 1933 in this bright, sunlit atelier, the Franciscan postulant Berta Hummel worked on her projects.

Her first project, as a visiting art teacher to the school administered at Saulgau, was a strenuous one, and no doubt Berta Hummel was always glad to return to the Motherhouse to work in her studio. She also taught art at the Convent-run school on the Siessen grounds. The local children took a quick liking to the ebullient young postulant,

and some of them would take their Sunday afternoon strolls out to Siessen to visit her. Their reward for the two-mile walk would sometimes be a Hummel sketch. As adults, many of Sister Maria Innocentia's former pupils still make that same walk today.

Another major undertaking of Berta Hummel during her time as a Franciscan postulant was the design of religious vestments and banners, an area in which the Siessen Convent had earned a wide reputation. Applying her talents to further the Convent's long-standing tradition in this field, Berta Hummel saw her concepts in this area reach as far as Africa and Brazil. Some of her designs bore angelic motifs, others included the faces of various saints including Saint Francis, the patron of the Franciscan Order. The vestments and banners, some of them embroidered in fine Japanese gold thread, required an average of 1,000 hours to complete. Still, the quick sketching technique that Berta Hummel mastered at the Munich Academy continued to win the hearts of the young children in her art classes. This, combined with the painstaking work on the religious motifs of the banners and vestments, served to fuse her talents and direct them toward a new phase of artistic development.

"When Sister Innocentia first arrived at the Convent she was searching for artistic direction," Sister Candalicia, one of the Franciscan Sisters who knew Sister Innocentia at Siessen, said. "She had not yet found her real style, but continued sketching and designing of vestments helped."

According to Sister Berta, another of the Franciscan Sisters who knew Sister Innocentia, the initial impetus to create the sketches which would later become "M.I. Hummel" figurines developed as the result of Berta Hummel's work on her projects. "She had so much energy and a wonderful sense of humor," Sister Berta said.

Berta Hummel's quick wit and marvelous sense of humor did not dull a bit from its sharpness of her Munich Academy days, largely because she used these traits in establishing the teacher-pupil rapport essential for the teaching of kindergarten and grade school. After being given her habit as a member of the Third Order of Saint Francis, Sister Maria Innocentia Hummel created a series of drawings, designed to amuse and reward the young children she was teaching. In November 1933, she took these drawings to a symposium of both lay and religious kindergarten teachers which was being held in the town of Rottenberg am Neckar.

"The drawings were very well received by the symposium," Sister Candalicia recalled, "and this acceptance gave Sister Innocentia an important feeling of confidence in her work."

As result of this modest acclaim, the name of Sister Maria Innocentia Hummel became so known that several art publishers were vying to distribute her work. By the summer of 1934, Sister Maria Innocentia Hummel's work was already appearing throughout Germany in the form of postcards, not to mention her collaboration with authoress Margareta Seeman on a children's book entitled, *The Hummel Book.* All of Sister Innocentia's artwork still is administered by the Siessen Convent, which grants licenses and charges royalty fees for the right to publish Sister Innocentia's artwork in forms which it sees befitting.

Sister Maria Innocentia Hummel illuminated happiness for her fellow Sisters to reflect upon, too. Her period as a postulant had taught her not only to express herself through the spirit of Saint Francis, but to provide joy to those immediately around her as well. One of the sisters of the Siessen Convent, who first met Sister Innocentia in 1933, recalled an incident in which a fellow sister was particularly sad: "When Sister Innocentia saw the sister's sadness, she glanced at her for a moment and then quietly scurried off to her studio. Later in the day she came to the saddened sister with the sketch of a little duck, bearing the caption *'Kopf hoch und schlucken,'* ('keep your head high and

swallow'). Soon the unhappy sister was in a much better mood." Later, the same sketch would appear in *The Hummel Book*, first published by Emil Finck Verlag in 1934. "Sister Innocentia's wonderful humor and willingness to help others brightened the atmosphere of our Convent," Mother Superior added. "The feeling of innocence and veneration that are present in her artwork are true Franciscan traits."

The bright-eyed smiles of the children in Sister Innocentia's sketches and the guiltless faces of her little angels and Madonnas were unsoiled by the Aryan themes that were being pushed by the propaganda machine of Herr Dr. Goebbels. For many Germans, 1933 was a year of hard times. Adolf Hitler had won power from the caretaker government of an aging von Hindenburg. The theories of Nazism were no longer hot air rising above the crowds in the smoke-clouded beer halls of Munich; they were an overwhelming reality. The work of a humble Franciscan Sister would soon be tantamount to a David, offering a joyous spirit to the soul of a nation, which, in fear of communism, deferred to national socialism and the mustering call of its goliath Third Reich.

But the appeal of the new order was slow in rallying the German artisans. Speedy programs of economic recovery from unemployment and inflation favored the heavy industries, holding large sectors of Bavaria and Thuringia, whose economies depended in large part on the production of porcelain and figurines, in relative disregard.

One of the firms experiencing a slow recovery was the W. Goebel *Porzellanfabrik* in Oeslau, a small town some five miles east of the city of Coburg. The Goebel firm history stemmed from a license to manufacture porcelain and related products granted by the Dukes of Saxe-Coburg-Gotha in 1871. A family-owned company in its fourth generation of proud tradition, the W. Goebel firm employed 350 workers when Franz Goebel first saw the sketches of Sister Maria Innocentia Hummel in 1934.

With a bleak economic outlook, Oeslau, like the other porcelain towns of Germany, was worried. Layoffs at the Goebel factory were imminent, and for Franz Goebel, it would have been a sad day in both the town and company histories if he had had to send those who had devoted lifetimes to the firm into the ranks of the unemployed. Like his father and grandfather, Franz Goebel knew the American market's tastes in porcelain and figurines, and he had lived for short periods in Canada and the United States prior to assuming leadership of the family business. The concept of making the sketches of Sister Maria Innocentia Hummel into ceramic figurines for the export market rang true as one which could bring a much needed economic upswing to his company and the town as well.

Late in 1934 Franz Goebel journeyed to Siessen to share his figurine idea with the Convent in the hope that they would grant him permission to manufacture ceramic figurines from Sister Innocentia's art. At first Sister Innocentia expressed reluctance, but in ensuing discussions both Sister Maria Innocentia Hummel and the Siessen Convent agreed to permit the W. Goebel firm to manufacture ceramic figurines from her two-dimensional artworks, the Convent holding final approval of all figurine designs before they reached the marketplace, just as it does today.

During the winter of 1934-35, Sister Maria Innocentia Hummel made her frist trip to the town of Oeslau to advise the W. Goebel craftsmen in the manufacture of figurines based on her artworks. She paid particular attention to color, delicately correcting the blending of special ceramic paints to conform with the colors of her drawings. On other occasions during this development period, artists of the Goebel firm and Franz Goebel himself journeyed to Siessen to hold conferences and present final models for approval. In March 1935, the first "M.I. Hummel" figurines were put on display for export at the Leipzig Trade Fair. The trademark and name "M.I. Hummel," protected internationally, reflects the fact that the figurines are made from the artwork of Sister Maria Innocentia Hummel created during her life as a religious after entering the Siessen Convent on April 22, 1931, and manufactured as three-dimensional ceramic figurines by the W. Goebel firm under an exclusive licensing agreement with the Siessen Convent.

The first "M.I. Hummel" figurines arrived in America in May 1935, and were accepted by the American collectors' market with enough success to warrant W. Goebel's considering the manufacture of new designs based on Sister Innocentia's sketches. These original seven "M.I. Hummel" figurines, models HUM 1 through HUM 10, include some of the most popular and sought-after models on the collecting scene today.

Those who had expressed disappointment over the departure of Berta Hummel from the Munich Academy of Applied Arts in 1931 were happy to see Sister Maria Innocentia Hummel return to the Academy in the fall of 1935. She began a graduate curriculum that centered on painting, and, as a result, spent a great deal of time around the famous museums of Munich, including the *Alte Pinakothek*, studying the masters of the 17th and 18th centuries. She worked in color, chalk, watercolor, charcoal, and oil, experimenting with color and composition. But most of all, Sister Maria Innocentia Hummel continued to perfect her own personal style, best reflected in the "M.I. Hummel" figurines.

During 1936, the demand on the export market was so great that Franz Goebel asked the Siessen Convent for permission to make several new figurines from the artwork of Sister Innocentia. "M.I. Hummel" figurines were a surprising success in America, and one of the biggest outlets for them at the time was the Marshall Field Company of Chicago, the largest department store in the Midwest. Both the Siessen Convent and Sister Innocentia were in accord, and once again a lively exchange took place between Oeslau and Siessen.

Sister Maria Innocentia Hummel continued to make visits to W. Goebel in Oeslau to inspect the models of her designs and oversee the various production steps in the figurine manufacture to ensure conformity with her artwork. Occasionally Sister Innocentia would suggest a minor change, the brightening of a color, or the positioning of a hat or an umbrella that would conform the figurine to her original artwork and make it more attractive to the collector's eye. The precedents of strict quality control and design review came about due to the excellent working relationship between Franz Goebel and Sister Maria Innocentia Hummel. They are precedents which continue at the Goebel firm today, precedents that have been responsible for the initiation of occasional minor changes in the figurines, often referred to by collectors as "model variations." These will be discussed later in a special chapter.

Unfortunately, Sister Innocentia's second sojourn to Munich was short-lived. She was very busy studying, painting, and drawing during 1936, making trips to Oeslau to supervise the manufacture of "M.I. Hummel" figurines as well. During the fall, she contracted a bad case of the flu and had to withdraw from her advanced studies at the Munich Academy in order to rest and recuperate at the Siessen Motherhouse.

"Sister Innocentia was about five feet six," Sister Cantalicia remembered, "but very thin. She was very energetic, always darting through the halls of the Convent." The ever-present energy was her trademark, typified by the busy little bees she often drew buzzing around her sketches. But in spite of her energy and fervent devotion to God, Sister Innocentia had to make an adjustment in her life.

INNOCENTIA HUMMEL (1909-1946)

Few woman artists of our day are likely to carry their art to the people in the manner that Sister Innocentia Hummel (Order of Saint Francis) has. Millions of her colorful greeting cards take joy from house to house, and prints of her paintings hang proudly in many homes and businesses. Sister Innocentia has cleverly designed innumerable variations on the theme of joyful, playing children, fresh and roguish as if they had strayed from their mother's watchful eye. The gift of her art was this priceless endowment of joy, radiating a spirit with which everyone can identify.

The call to Heaven will not take Innocentia Hummel's art. For it will always rest on the horizon. It is a testament to her deep feelings, rising with passion to send her message to the people. Her popularity increased even further after her children's sketches were sculpted into ceramic figurines. And in keeping with her Lower Bavarian traditions, Sister Innocentia Hummel took this success in a most quiet and soft-spoken manner.

In the foreground of her life, this youthful Franciscan Sister always stood ready and willing to help others. Those who knew her often had outward apprehensions about her long hours and frail body, but she commanded her talents courageously and each artistic work streamed from her like a song. She once said: "Man must have a light heart (or, translated in another manner, man must be light-hearted) to live beyond his difficulties."

Her life was not without tests. Religious life demanded many sacrifices from her. Her sunny humor was not inherited from her family tradition, but from sacrifice and devotion to God. Innocentia Hummel had a heart which never felt the necessity to say no.

Sister Innocentia Hummel came, as did Brother Konrad von Parzahm, from the valley of the River Rott in Lower Bavaria. An ancestor was the priest and artist Dominikus Hummel (1769-1800). Her father, a merchant. Of six brothers and sisters, she was the third eldest. Beginning in 1921, she attended the Institute of English Sisters in Simbach. In 1927, she began her studies at the Academy for Applied Arts in Munich. She lived with the Sisters of the Holy Family in Blumenstrasse 10. While attending her art classes, she met two Franciscan Sisters from the convent Siessen-Saulgau. After passing her state examination in 1931, she went into seclusion. On August 30, 1934, she was formally inducted into the Franciscan Order.

Shortly thereafter, two books featuring her artwork appeared: *Das Hummel-buch*, by Margareta Seeman (Emil Fink Verlag, Stuttgart, 1934); and a collection of short story illustrations, *Hui, die Hummel*, (Ars-Sacra/Josef Muller Verlag, Munchen). These works reflect the stroke of confidence she had accrued in her descriptions of the children's world.

During her last ten years, the scope of her art broadened. She was commissioned to design altars and murals. The altar painting of Brother Konrad in Saint Stephen's Church in Massing shows her own personal concentration and revelation in the personification of God. One is seized by the deep intimacy that beams from her "Mural of Piety" in Tuttlingen. This work saw her beat a new path, and a style one would hardly expect from an artist such as Sister Innocentia. Her desire for a massive undertaking was rewarded when she was commissioned to design the interior of the cathedral in the Bavarian town of Rathmannsdorf. Sister Innocentia was given the opportunity to spread the tradition of German Catholic art into Africa, but she spurned the offer of the Marienhilfe missionary society, remaining true to her own visions.

It is regrettable that many critics place religious art outside the world of art and culture. Sister Innocentia's exhibitions in the summer of 1946 in Saulgau, and in Friedrichshafen show the many facets and directions of her efforts and prove that the main of the critics have taken a false approach. Her clarity in graphic design brought us religious vestments and wall tapestries, too. Through her expert art pedagogy, she passed her talents on to her co-workers, Sister Laura Brugger and Sister Kostka. On November 6, 1946, the Siessen Convent lost their beloved sister at the very moment the chapel bells tolled noon.

Hugo Schnell

Notes: This obituary is publicly obtainable—extractable from the reference library, fourth floor, Academy of Fine Arts, Akademiestrasse 2, Munchen 40. The bound volume is not removable.

It appeared in the Catholic magazine for art and art history, *Das Munster*, issue spring-fall 1947, published by Verlag Schnell & Steiner, Munich (first year of publication after World War II).

CHAPTER
4: THE FINAL YEARS

Sister Maria Innocentia Hummel.

From 1937 to 1939, Sister Maria Innocentia Hummel's resistance seemed to have lowered. She always had a cold or a flu, and as a result she spent most of her time at work in her studio. At harvest time, when the rest of the Convent would take to the fields, Sister Innocentia was told that she could best serve her fellow sisters from her atelier, letting her spirit partake through her art. By September 1939, Sister Innocentia's strength had not improved. Still, she persevered and garnered the spirit to continue with her artistic pursuits in spite of the Nazi-imposed hardships that so disturbed Convent life. She created countless sketches, some of which were made into "M.I. Hummel" figurines, earning the royalties from the W. Goebel firm that enabled the Siessen Convent to exist in spite of governmental repression. Sister Maria Innocentia Hummel had not yet felt the real mood of the war, nor did she realize that it would put her body and soul to their utmost test.

On February 6, 1937, the Nazi government issued a decree that all Catholic administered schools and other private schools would be systematically closed. At the same time, Berlin raised the taxes of all convents to create a severe economic burden, hoping that institutions like Siessen, with long and proud educational traditions, would eventually collapse. Sister Maria Innocentia Hummel continued her artwork at Siessen during this period. The manufacture of "M.I. Hummel" figurines and the subsequent royalties paid Siessen by the Goebel firm helped the Convent to overcome those hardships.

It was 1940, era of the Battle of Britain and the Russian Front. The Berlin government issued a decree that all religious activities in Germany be stopped. On October 31, 1940, Kreisleiter Siller, the local Nazi district leader of Saulgau, and Kreisleiter Drautz of Heilbronn, accompanied by officers of the feared SS, brought SS orders that from that day forth the Siessen Motherhouse would be transformed into an ethnic repatriation center for Germans who had formerly lived in Russia, Romania, Yugoslavia, and Slovenia. Everyone was ordered to leave with their belongings in eight days.

"Send the sisters home," Kreisleiter Drautz told the leaders and administrators of the Convent, the Convent's history book remembers. "Their Jesus will provide for them."

Relatives of the Siessen Sisters came from far and wide in automobiles or on trains to help take the Convent's belongings away. Sister Innocentia, like the rest of the Siessen Sisters, reluctantly left the Convent and joined her family in Massing.

"We knew of the hardships," ninety-year-old Viktoria Hummel said, "but we didn't think that Berta would be coming home. She was welcome and we were glad to see her, but all she talked about was going back to the Convent."

Brother Adolf and sister Centa were also very happy to see their sister, but even then her health was in obvious decline. Three weeks after being expelled by the Nazis, Sister Maria Innocentia Hummel received permission to return to the Convent. A few sisters were needed to care for the sick and to perform administrative tasks. "She went back," Centa said of her sister, "because the Convent was her home and her life."

On December 8, 1940, the first 400 repatriated Germans came to Siessen Convent. Eventually that number would jump to 2,000. Sister Innocentia, forced to give up her studio, lived in a damp basement room that also served as her work area.

On January 13, 1941, sensing Catholic sympathies among the refugees, Kreisleiter Drautz of Heilbronn used his power to expropriate all of the Siessen-owned farmland in the name of the Third Reich, to conform with the government food program. All crop harvesting and animal slaughtering, therefore, came under the aegis of the military police, and on July 10, 1941, the local Nazi leaders accused the remaining few Franciscan Sisters of con-

Sister Maria Innocentia Hummel's sketch of madonna and child that became the basis for HUM 48 Madonna Plaque.

The close relationship between Franz Goebel, Sister Maria Innocentia Hummel and the Siessen Convent is emphasized by this 1936 photo taken at the Goebel factory gardens. At left is the Mother Superior of the Siessen Convent, Franz Goebel is in the center and Sister M.I. Hummel at the right.

spiring to use more food than the war plan allowed. Wary of the Franciscan tradition of helping the poor, the Nazis tightened their control over all food produced at Siessen. As a result, the remaining sisters and the refugees lived in virtual famine while the Nazis reaped the bounty of the crops.

The grave food shortages did little to bolster the resistance of Sister Maria Innocentia Hummel, who, in spite of the cramped conditions, continued to sketch with the hope that others would obtain a feeling of veneration from her art. New restrictions were put on firewood and coal, and Sister Innocentia, working in her damp little room, developed complications to a cold which were first diagnosed as pleurisy, later as a lung infection. There were no antibiotics available due to the war effort, nor were there any specialists to look after Sister Innocentia's problem. She underwent a series of chest X-rays in 1940 which tested out negative, but she was still required to spend several weeks recuperating at the Motherhouse.

By the spring of 1941, Sister Maria Innocentia Hummel was once again spending her Sunday afternoons out-of-doors, sketching local children and bringing a priceless quality of joy into the lives of the sisters and the refugees who lived under the siege of Nazism.

In the fall of 1944, Sister Innocentia suffered a relapse of her lung infection, and after she was sent to Wilhelmstift, a hospital at Isny in the Swabian Alps, it was found that her earlier X-rays had been incorrectly read and that, in fact, her condition should have been diagnosed as chronic tuberculosis. She was given the opportunity to travel to neutral Switzerland where she would have received superlative medical attention and had a much better chance for speedy recovery. But she refused to travel alone, and additional travel documents were unavailable. Knowing the finality of her prognosis, Sister Maria Innocentia asked and was allowed to remain at the hospital.

Sister Innocentia tried to live as normal a life as possible, always in good humor and often making sketches to cheer up other patients around her. She decorated the X-ray laboratory so the doctors and technicians would have something more cheerful to look at than wet readings and sore spots. Her reputation known to many at the hospital, Sister Innocentia used only the simple name Maria upon her room door.

On April 11, 1945, the Second World War all but over, Sister Maria Innocentia Hummel departed the hospital sufficiently recovered to return to the Motherhouse. French troops had occupied the area of southwestern Germany surrounding Siessen, and when on April 22, 1945, the town of Saulgau and the Convent were liberated by the French forces, Sister Innocentia returned to Siessen.

By November 1945 she had suffered a relapse. Sister Maria Innocentia Hummel was sent to a Franciscan sanatorium at the town of Wangen, but her condition continued to deteriorate, later becoming complicated by dropsy. Wanting to spend her last days at the Motherhouse, Sister Innocentia was brought to Siessen in September 1946. At noon, on November 6, 1946, the same chapel bells that stood witness to the siege of Nazism tolled out the message that Sister Maria Innocentia Hummel was dead.

CHAPTER
5: THE NAME LIVES ON

When the United States Army occupied the city of Coburg and its surrounding area, production at the W. Goebel firm had already ground to a halt. The firm had contributed to the home front production effort by manufacturing dinnerware of a ceramic nature and a small amount of fine china. Coffee mugs and mess hall plates had been produced for the war effort. But with the collapse of the Third Reich there were not even these orders to be filled. Like all German industry, W. Goebel was on the verge of collapse, but a quirk of political history worked in favor of its fate.

According to the lines drawn up by the four-power treaty at the end of the Second World War, the city of Coburg and the town of Oeslau, location of the Goebel firm, were left in a pocket, surrounded on three sides by communist East Germany and completely cut off from their historic lines of commercial influence. Committed to developing the economy of the border region, the U.S. Military Government quickly lifted the wartime embargo and granted the W. Goebel firm a permit to manufacture and export "M.I. Hummel" figurines and other collectors items. Some of the first postwar collectors were the GIs stationed in Germany with the American occupation forces.

By 1949 the Federal Republic of Germany had been formed, the Marshall Plan was sparking reconstruction, and production at W. Goebel was in full swing. Factory worker strength was at an all time high of 800. The combination of prewar collectors anxious to acquire new figurines, ex-GIs and their families, and civilian employees of the U.S. Government who were spending tours of duty in Germany brought continued collector interest on the home front. At the same time, the constantly rotating army of soldiers of the occupation force discovered the "M.I. Hummel" experience in West Germany and brought the figurines back home.

For the American GIs stationed in West Germany, Hummel figurine collecting was an inexpensive and constructive pastime that broke the droll monotony of restrictive barracks life. GIs on weekend passes and increasing numbers of American tourists would scour German towns for "M.I. Hummel" figurines, building their collections and above all using the common interest in collecting to spread goodwill and better German-American relations.

In this reconstruction era of black-market food and irregular currency speculation, Hummel figurines were often purchasable at what would be considered extreme bargain prices by today's standards. Until the summer of 1958, the U.S. Army in Germany paid its troops in Military Payment Certificates (MPC)—similar to the system used in Viet Nam—in an attempt to keep U.S. dollars off the German black market. GIs could exchange these MPC at military banking facilities at a fixed rate of exchange—approximately 4.75 German marks for every dollar—but they always found a more lucrative exchange with the German taxi drivers, who paid at a rate of six marks to each U.S. MPC dollar. Tourists with real greenbacks found an even higher rate of exchange.

Through shrewd currency bargaining, GIs and tourists could purchase their Hummel figurines at normal retail price, in reality paying only one-half to two-thirds the cost due to the unofficial rates of exchange. In July 1958, the U.S. Army called in all of its

The W. Goebel factory in 1914.

MPC and began paying the troops in greenbacks. Exchange rates stabilized somewhat, but with more greenbacks and collectors floating around Germany, "Hummel fever" continued, giving birth to countless collections of figurines that are very difficult to find today.

Though U.S. servicemen and American tourists in Europe helped broaden "M.I. Hummel" collecting interest, the Hummel experience is shared by the broadest spectrum of American society. With millions of collectors in the United States alone, Hummel collecting has become one of America's national pastimes. The U.S. government recognized this in 1952 when the Treasury Department designated "M.I. Hummel" figurines as works of art.

CHAPTER 6: THE COLLECTION

Here is the first fully authorized documentation of the complete collection of "M.I. Hummel" figurines photographed from W. Goebel's factory archive collection in Rödental, West Germany, including detailed notes on every figurine ever made.

This list, compiled from the W. Goebel production journal in Rödental, West Germany, constitutes a record of all "M.I. Hummel" figurines that have been authorized for production. "M.I. Hummel" figurine identification numbers run in ascending order from 1 to 396. English and German names of the figurines as well as their sizes and notes on most models will be found in the special annotated listing.

All sizes are approximate and depend upon exact method of measurement. Minor variations occur frequently and therefore should not be considered significant.

"M.I. Hummel" figurine identification numbers and their corresponding figurines are divided into four distinct categories:

Open Edition (OE): Pieces currently in W. Goebel's production program.

Closed Edition (CE): Pieces formerly in W. Goebel's production program but no longer produced. These pieces will never be produced again.

Though all closed editions are noted in the annotated listing, not all of them are photographically shown in the gallery section.

Open Number (ON): An identification number, which in W. Goebel's numerical identification system has not yet been used, but which may be used to identify new "M.I. Hummel" figurines as they are released in the future.

Closed Number (CN): A number which has not been used and will not be used to identify an "M.I. Hummel" figurine.

HUM No.	NAME	SIZE	STATUS
1	**"Puppy Love"**/*"Geigerlein" mit Hund*	5″	OE
2/0	**"Little Fiddler"**/*"Geigerlein" ohne Hund*	6″	OE
2/I	**"Little Fiddler"**/*"Geigerlein" ohne Hund*	7½″	OE
2/II	**"Little Fiddler"**/*"Geigerlein" ohne Hund*	10¾″	OE
2/III	**"Little Fiddler"**/*"Geigerlein" ohne Hund*	12¼″	OE
3/I	**"Book Worm"**/*"Der Bücherwurm"*	5½″	OE
3/II	**"Book Worm"**/*"Der Bücherwurm"*	8″	OE
3/III	**"Book Worm"**/*"Der Bücherwurm"*	9″	OE
4	**"Little Fiddler"**/*"Geigerlein" ohne Hund*	4¾″	OE
5	**"Strolling Along"**/*"Wanderbub" mit Hund*	4¾″	OE
6/0	**"Sensitive Hunter"**/*"Jägerlein"*	4¾″	OE
6/I	**"Sensitive Hunter"**/*"Jägerlein"*	5½″	OE
6/II	**"Sensitive Hunter"**/*"Jägerlein"*	7½″	OE
7/0	**"Merry Wanderer"**/*"Wanderbub" ohne Hund*	6¼″	OE
7/I	**"Merry Wanderer"**/*"Wanderbub" ohne Hund*	7″	OE
7/II	**"Merry Wanderer"**/*"Wanderbub" ohne Hund*	9½″	OE
7/III	**"Merry Wanderer"**/*"Wanderbub" ohne Hund*	11¼″	OE
8	**"Book Worm"**/*"Der Bücherwurm"*	4″	OE
9	**"Begging his Share"**/*"Gratulant"*	5½″	OE
10/I/W	**Flower Madonna**/*Blumen-Madonna mit Kind*	8¼″	OE
10/I/11	**Flower Madonna**/*Blumen-Madonna mit Kind*	8¼″	OE
10/III/W	**Flower Madonna**/*Blumen-Madonna mit Kind*	11½″	OE
10/III/11	**Flower Madonna**/*Blumen-Madonna mit Kind*	11½″	OE
11/2/0	**Merry Wanderer**/*Wanderbub ohne Hund*	4¼″	OE
11/0	**Merry Wanderer**/*Wanderbub ohne Hund*	4¾″	OE
12/2/0	**Chimney Sweep**/*"Ich bringe Glück," Kaminfeger*	4″	OE
12/I	**Chimney Sweep**/*"Ich bringe Glück," Kaminfeger*	5½″	OE
13/2/0	**Meditation**/*Die Gratulantin*	4¼″	OE
13/0	**Meditation**/*Die Gratulantin*	5½″	OE
13/II	**Meditation**/*Die Gratulantin*	7″	OE
13/V	**Meditation**/*Die Gratulantin*	13¾″	OE
14/A&B	**Book Worm, Book Ends, Boy and Girl**/*Der Bücherwurm, Buchstütze Junge und Mädchen*	5½″	OE
15/0	**Hear Ye, Hear Ye**/*"Hört Ihr Leute," Nachtwächter*	5″	OE
15/I	**Hear Ye, Hear Ye**/*"Hört Ihr Leute," Nachtwächter*	6″	OE

HUM No.	NAME	SIZE	STATUS
15/II	**Hear Ye, Hear Ye**/*"Hört Ihr Leute," Nachtwächter*	7"	OE
16/2/0	**Little Hiker**/*Hans im Glück*	4½"	OE
16/I	**Little Hiker**/*Hans im Glück*	6"	OE
17	**Congratulations**/*Ich gratuliere*	6"	OE
18	**Christ Child**/*Stille Nacht, Jesuskind*	2 x 6"	OE
19			CN
20	**Prayer before Battle**/*Der fromme Reitersmann*	4¼"	OE
21/0	**Heavenly Angel**/*Christkindlein kommt, Engel*	4¾"	OE
21/0/½	**Heavenly Angel**/*Christkindlein kommt, Engel*	6¾"	OE
21/II	**Heavenly Angel**/*Christkindlein kommt, Engel*	8¾"	OE
22/0	**Holy Water Font, Sitting Angel**/*Weihkessel, sitzender Engel*	2¾ x 3½"	OE
22/I	**Holy Water Font, Sitting Angel**/*Weihkessel, sitzender Engel*	3¼ x 4"	OE
23/I	**Adoration**/*Bei Mutter Maria, Marterl*	6¼"	OE
23/III	**Adoration**/*Bei Mutter Maria, Marterl*	9"	OE
24/I	**Lullaby**/*Wiegenlied*	3½ x 5"	OE
24/III	**Lullaby**/*Wiegenlied*	6 x 8"	OE
25	**Angelic Sleep**/*Stille Nacht*	3½ x 5"	OE
26/I	**Holy Water Font, Child Jesus**/*Weihkessel*	2½ x 6"	OE
26/0	**Holy Water Font, Child Jesus**/*Weihkessel*	1½ x 5"	OE
27/III	**Joyous News**/*O, du fröliche*	4¼ x 4¾"	OE
28/II	**Wayside Devotion**/*Abendlied, Marterl*	7½"	OE
28/III	**Wayside Devotion**/*Abendlied, Marterl*	8¾"	OE
29	**Holy Water Font, Guardian Angel**/*Weihkessel*	2½ x 5¾"	CE
29/0	**Holy Water Font, Guardian Angel**/*Weihkessel*	2⅜ x 6"	CE
30/A&B	**Ba-Bee Ring**/*Hui, die Hummel, Wandring*	4¾ x 5"	OE
31	**Advent Group with Candle**/*Adventsgruppe mit Kerzen*		CE
32/0	**Little Gabriel**/*O, du fröhliche . . . , Engel*	5"	OE
33	**Ashtray, Joyful**/*Gesangsprobe, Ascher*	3½ x 6"	OE
34	**Ashtray, Singing Lesson**/*'s stimmt net, Ascher*	3½ x 6¼"	OE
35/0	**Holy Water Font, The Good Shepherd**/*Der gute Hirte, Weihkessel*	2¼ x 4¾"	OE
35/I	**Holy Water Font, The Good Shepherd**/*Der gute Hirte, Weihkessel*	2¾ x 5¾"	OE
36/0	**Holy Water Font**/*Weihkessel, sitzender Engel*	2¾ x 4"	OE
36/I	**Holy Water Font**/*Weihkessel, sitzender Engel*	3½ x 4½"	OE
37	**Herald Angels, Candlestick**/*Adventsleuchter mit 3 Engeln*	2½ x 4"	OE
I/38/0	**Angel, Joyous News, with Lute, Candleholder**/*Adventsengelchen mit Laute*	2"	OE
III/38/0	**Angel, Joyous News, with Lute, Candleholder**/*Adventsengelchen mit Laute*	2"	OE
III/38/I	**Angel, Joyous News, with Lute, Candleholder**/*Adventsengelchen mit Laute*	2¾"	OE
I/39/0	**Angel, Joyous News, with Accordion, Candleholder**/*Adventsengelchen mit Bandoneon*	2"	OE
III/39/0	**Angel, Joyous News, with Accordion, Candleholder**/*Adventsengelchen mit Bandoneon*	2"	OE
III/39/I	**Angel, Joyous News, with Accordion, Candleholder**/*Adventsengelchen mit Bandoneon*	2¾"	OE
I/40/0	**Angel, Joyous News, with Trumpet, Candleholder**/*Adventsengelchen mit Trompete*	2"	OE
III/40/0	**Angel, Joyous News, with Trumpet, Candleholder**/*Adventsengelchen mit Trompete*	2"	OE
III/40/I	**Angel, Joyous News, with Trumpet, Candleholder**/*Adventsengelchen mit Trompete*	2¾"	OE
41			CN
42	**Good Shepherd**/*Der gute Hirte*	6¼"	OE
43	**March Winds**/*Lausbub*	5"	OE
44/A	**Culprits, Table Lamp**	8½"	OE
44/B	**Out of Danger, Table Lamp**	8½"	OE
45/0/W	**Madonna with halo**/*Madonna mit Heiligenschein*	10½"	OE
45/0/6	**Madonna with halo**/*Madonna mit Heiligenschein*	10½"	OE
45/0/13	**Madonna with halo**/*Madonna mit Heiligenschein*	10½"	OE

HUM No.	NAME	SIZE	STATUS
45/I/W	**Madonna with halo**/*Madonna mit Heiligenschein*	12″	**OE**
45/I/6	**Madonna with halo**/*Madonna mit Heiligenschein*	12″	**OE**
45/I/13	**Madonna with halo**/*Madonna mit Heiligenschein*	12″	**OE**
45/III/W	**Madonna with halo**/*Madonna mit Heiligenschein*	16¾″	**OE**
45/III/6	**Madonna with halo**/*Madonna mit Heiligenschein*	16¾″	**OE**
45/III/13	**Madonna with halo**/*Madonna mit Heiligenschein*	16¾″	**OE**
46/0/W	**Madonna without halo**/*Madonna ohne Heiligenschein*	10¼″	**OE**
46/0/6	**Madonna without halo**/*Madonna ohne Heiligenschein*	10¼″	**OE**
46/0/13	**Madonna without halo**/*Madonna ohne Heiligenschein*	10¼″	**OE**
46/I/W	**Madonna without halo**/*Madonna ohne Heiligenschein*	11¼″	**OE**
46/I/6	**Madonna without halo**/*Madonna ohne Heiligenschein*	11¼″	**OE**
46/I/13	**Madonna without halo**/*Madonna ohne Heiligenschein*	11¼″	**OE**
46/III/W	**Madonna without halo**/*Madonna ohne Heiligenschein*	16¼″	**OE**
46/III/6	**Madonna without halo**/*Madonna ohne Heiligenschein*	16¼″	**OE**
46/III/13	**Madonna without halo**/*Madonna ohne Heiligenschein*	16¼″	**OE**
47/3/0	**Goose Girl**/*Gänseliesl*	4″	**OE**
47/0	**Goose Girl**/*Gänseliesl*	4¾″	**OE**
47/II	**Goose Girl**/*Gänseliesl*	7½″	**OE**
48/0	**Madonna Plaque**/*Madonnenbild*	3 x 4″	**OE**
48/II	**Madonna Plaque**/*Madonnenbild*	4¾ x 6″	**OE**
49/3/0	**To Market**/*Brüderlein und Schwesterlein*	4″	**OE**
49/0	**To Market**/*Brüderlein und Schwesterlein*	5½″	**OE**
49/I	**To Market**/*Brüderlein und Schwesterlein*	6¼″	**OE**
50/2/0	**Volunteers**/*Soldatenspiel*	5″	**OE**
50/0	**Volunteers**/*Soldatenspiel*	5½″	**OE**
50/I	**Volunteers**/*Soldatenspiel*	6½″	**OE**
51/3/0	**Village Boy**/*Dorfbub*	4″	**OE**
51/2/0	**Village Boy**/*Dorfbub*	5″	**OE**
51/0	**Village Boy**/*Dorfbub*	6″	**OE**
51/I	**Village Boy**/*Dorfbub*	7¼″	**OE**
52/0	**Going to Grandma's**/*Hausmütterchen*	4¾″	**OE**
52/I	**Going to Grandma's**/*Hausmütterchen*	6″	**OE**
53	**Joyful**/*Gesangsprobe*	4″	**OE**
III/53	**Joyful, Box**/*Gesangsprobe, Dose*	6″	**OE**
54	**Silent Night**/*Stille Nacht, Krippe*	5½ x 4¾″	**OE**
55	**Saint George**/*Ritter Heilige Georg*	6¾″	**OE**
56/A	**Culprits**/*Apfeldieb, Junge*	6¼″	**OE**
56/B	**Out of Danger**/*In Sicherheit, Mädchen*	6¼″	**OE**
57/0	**Chick Girl**/*Kückenmütterchen*	3½″	**OE**
57/I	**Chick Girl**/*Kückenmütterchen*	4¼″	**OE**
III/57	**Chick Girl, Box**/*Kückenmütterchen, Dose*	6¼″	**OE**
58/0	**Playmates**/*Hasenvater*	4″	**OE**
58/I	**Playmates**/*Hasenvater*	4¼″	**OE**
III/58	**Playmates, Box**/*Hasenvater, Dose*	6¼″	**OE**
59	**Skier**/*Ski-heil*	5″	**OE**
60/A	**Book Ends: Farm Boy**/*Schweinhirt, Buchstützen*	4¾″	**OE**
60/B	**Book Ends: Goose Girl**/*Gänseliesl, Buchstützen*	4¾″	**OE**
61/A	**Book Ends: Playmates**/*Hasenvater, Buchstützen*	4″	**OE**
61/B	**Book Ends: Chick Girl**/*Kückenmütterchen, Buchstützen*	4″	**OE**
62	**Happy Pastime, Ashtray**/*Strickliesl, Ascher*	3½ x 6¼″	**OE**
63	**Singing Lesson**/*'s stimmt net*	2¾″	**OE**
III/63	**Singing Lesson, Box**/*'s stimmt net, Dose*	6″	**OE**
64	**Shepherd's Boy**/*Schäferbub*	5½″	**OE**
65	**Farewell**/*Auf Wiedersehen*	4¾″	**OE**
66	**Farm Boy**/*Schweinhirt*	5″	**OE**
67	**Doll Mother**/*Puppenmütterchen*	4¾″	**OE**
68/2/0	**Lost Sheep**/*Schäferbub*	4¼″	**OE**
68/0	**Lost Sheep**/*Schäferbub*	5½″	**OE**
69	**Happy Pastime**/*Strickliesl*	3½″	**OE**
III/69	**Happy Pastime, Box**/*Strickliesl, Dose*	6″	**OE**
70	**The Holy Child**/*Jesulein*	6¾″	**OE**
71	**Stormy Weather**/*Unter einem Dach*	6¼″	**OE**

HUM No.	NAME	SIZE	STATUS
72	**Spring Cheer**/*Frühling ist's*	5″	OE
73	**Little Helper**/*Fleissiges Lieschen*	4″	OE
74	**Little Gardener**/*Die kleine Gärtnerin*	4″	OE
75	**Holy Water Font, White Angel**/*Weihkessel, Weisser Engel*	1¾ x 3½″	OE
76/A&B	**Book Ends, Doll Mother & Prayer before Battle**		CE
77			CN
78/VIII/83	**Infant of Krumbad**/*Jesuskind, liegend*	13¼″	OE
78/VI/83	**Infant of Krumbad**/*Jesuskind, liegend*	10″	OE
78/V/83	**Infant of Krumbad**/*Jesuskind, liegend*	7¾″	OE
78/III/83	**Infant of Krumbad**/*Jesuskind, liegend*	5½″	OE
78/II/83	**Infant of Krumbad**/*Jesuskind, liegend*	3½″	OE
78/I/83	**Infant of Krumbad**/*Jesuskind, liegend*	2½″	OE
78/VIII/11	**Infant of Krumbad**/*Jesuskind, liegend*	13½″	OE
78/VI/11	**Infant of Krumbad**/*Jesuskind, liegend*	10″	OE
78/V/11	**Infant of Krumbad**/*Jesuskind, liegend*	7¾″	OE
78/III/11	**Infant of Krumbad**/*Jesuskind, liegend*	5¼″	OE
78/II/11	**Infant of Krumbad**/*Jesuskind, liegend*	3½″	OE
78/I/11	**Infant of Krumbad**/*Jesuskind, liegend*	2½″	OE
79	**Globe Trotter**/*Hinaus in die Ferne*	5″	OE
80	**Little Scholar**/*Erster Schulgang, Junge*	5½″	OE
81/2/0	**School Girl**/*Erster Schulgang, Mädchen*	4¼″	OE
81/0	**School Girl**/*Erster Schulgang, Mädchen*	5″	OE
82/2/0	**School Boy**/*Schulschwänzer, Junge*	4″	OE
82/0	**School Boy**/*Schulschwänzer, Junge*	5″	OE
82/II	**School Boy**/*Schulschwänzer, Junge*	7½″	OE
83	**Angel Serenade**/*Fromme Weisen*	5½″	OE
84/0	**Worship**/*Am Wegesrand, Bildstöckl*	5″	OE
84/V	**Worship**/*Am Wegesrand, Bildstöckl*	12¾″	OE
85/0	**Serenade**/*Ständchen, Junge mit Flöte*	4¾″	OE
85/II	**Serenade**/*Ständchen, Junge mit Flöte*	7½″	OE
86	**Happiness**/*Wanderlied, Mädchen*	4¾″	OE
87	**For Father**/*Fürs Vaterle, Rettichbub*	5½″	OE
88/II	**Heavenly Protection**/*Schutzenengel*	9″	OE
88/I	**Heavenly Protection**/*Schutzenengel*	6¾″	OE
89/I	**Little Cellist**/*Heimkehr, Bassgeiger*	6″	OE
89/II	**Little Cellist**/*Heimkehr, Bassgeiger*	7½″	OE
90/A&B	**Book Ends—Wayside Devotion & Adoration**		CE
91/A	**Holy Water Font, Angel looking left**/*Weihkessel, Engel links schauend*	2 x 4¾″	OE
91/B	**Holy Water Font, Angel looking right**/*Weihkessel, Engel rechts schauend*	2 x 4¾″	OE
92	**Merry Wanderer, Plaque**/*Wanderbub, Bild*	5 x 5½″	OE
93	**Little Fiddler, Plaque**/*Geigerlein, Bild*	5 x 5½″	OE
94/3/0	**Surprise**/*Hänsel und Gretel*	4″	OE
94/I	**Surprise**/*Hänsel und Gretel*	5½″	OE
95	**Brother**/*Dorfheld*	5½″	OE
96	**Little Shopper**/*Gretel*	4¾″	OE
97	**Trumpet Boy**/*Der kleine Musikant*	4¾″	OE
98/2/0	**Sister**/*Der erste Einkauf*	4¾″	OE
98/0	**Sister**/*Der erste Einkauf*	5½″	OE
99	**Eventide**/*Abendlied*	4¼ x 4¾″	OE
100	**Shrine—Table Lamp**/*Marterl—Lampenfuss mit Figur*	7½″	CE
101	**Table Lamp—To Market**		CE
102	**Table Lamp—Volunteers**		CE
103	**Table Lamp—Farewell**		CE
104	**Table Lamp—Wayside Devotion**		CE
105			CN
106	**Merry Wanderer, Plaque**		CE
107	**Little Fiddler, Plaque**		CE
108			CN
109/0	**Happy Traveller**/*Hinaus in die Ferne*	5″	OE

HUM No.	NAME	SIZE	STATUS
109/II	**Happy Traveller**/*Hinaus in die Ferne*	7½″	OE
110/0	**Let's Sing**/*Heini, Bandoneonspieler*	3″	OE
110/I	**Let's Sing**/*Heini, Bandoneonspieler*	4″	OE
III/110	**Let's Sing, Box**/*Heini, Bandoneonspieler, Dose*	6″	OE
111/3/0	**Wayside Harmony**/*Vaters G'scheitester*	4″	OE
111/1	**Wayside Harmony**/*Vaters G'scheitester*	5″	OE
112/3/0	**Just Resting**/*Mutters Liebste*	4″	OE
112/I	**Just Resting**/*Mutters Liebste*	5″	OE
113	**Heavenly Song**/*Stille Nacht, Adventsgruppe*	3½ x 4¾″	OE
114	**Let's Sing, Ashtray**/*Heini, Ascher*	3½ x 6¼″	OE
115	**Advent Candlestick: Girl with nosegay**/*Adventsleuchter: Mädchen mit Blumenstrauss*	3½″	OE
116	**Advent Candlestick: Girl with fir tree**/*Adventsluechter: Mädchen mit Tannenbaum*	3½″	OE
117	**Advent Candlestick: Boy with horse**/*Adventsleuchter: Junge mit Holzpferd*	3½″	OE
118	**Little Thrifty**/*Spar-Hummelchen*	5″	OE
119	**Postman**/*Eilbote*	5″	OE
120	**Joyful and Let's Sing (on wooden base)**		CE
121	**Wayside Harmony and Just Resting (on wooden base)**		CE
122	**Puppy Love, Serenade, and Happiness (on wooden base)**		CE
123	**Max and Moritz**/*Max und Moritz*	5″	OE
124/0	**Chef, Hello**	6¼″	OE
124/I	**Chef, Hello**	7″	OE
125	**Vacation-Time, Plaque**/*Ferienfreunde, Bild*	4 x 4¾″	OE
126	**Retreat to Safety, Plaque**/*Angsthase, Bild*	4¾ x 4¾″	OE
127	**Doctor**/*Puppendoktor*	4¾″	OE
128	**Baker**/*Der kleine Konditor*	4¾″	OE
129	**Band Leader**/*Herr Kappellmeister*	5″	OE
130	**Duet**/*Duett, Sängerpaar*	5″	OE
131	**Street Singer**/*Kammersänger*	5″	OE
132	**Star Gazer**/*Sterngucker*	4¾″	OE
133	**Mother's Helper**/*Mutters Stütze*	5″	OE
134	**Plaque "Quartet"**/*Bild "Das Quartett"*	6 x 6″	OE
135	**Soloist**/*Heldentenor*	4¾″	OE
136/I	**Friends**/*Gute Freunde*	5″	OE
136/V	**Friends**/*Gute Freunde*	10¾″	OE
137	**Wall Plaque, Child in Bed**/*Wandring, Kind im Bettchen*	2¾ x 2¾″	OE
138			CN
139	**Flitting Butterfly**/*Sitzendes Kind mit Schmetterling, Wandring*	2½ x 2½″	OE
140	**The mail is here, Plaque**/*Trara—die Post ist da, Bild*	4¼ x 6¼″	OE
141/3/0	**Apple Tree Girl**/*Frühling, Mädchen im Baum*	4″	OE
141/I	**Apple Tree Girl**/*Frühling, Mädchen im Baum*	6″	OE
141/V	**Apple Tree Girl**/*Frühling, Mädchen im Baum*	10″	OE
141/X	**Apple Tree Girl**/*Frühling, Mädchen im Baum*	28″	OE
142/3/0	**Apple Tree Boy**/*Herbst, Junge im Baum*	4″	OE
142/I	**Apple Tree Boy**/*Herbst, Junge im Baum*	6″	OE
142/V	**Apple Tree Boy**/*Herbst, Junge im Baum*	10″	OE
142/X	**Apple Tree Boy**/*Herbst, Junge im Baum*	28″	OE
143/0	**Boots**/*Meister Wichtig*	5½″	OE
143/I	**Boots**/*Meister Wichtig*	6½″	OE
144	**Angelic Song**/*Singendes Kind mit Engelein*	4″	OE
145	**"Little Guardian"**/*Betendes Kind mit Engelein*	4″	OE
146	**Holy Water Font, Angel Duet**/*Weihkessel, Engelgrüppchen*	3¼ x 4¼″	OE
147	**Holy Water Font, Angel Shrine**/*Weihkessel, Engel*	3 x 5″	OE
148			CN
149			CN
150/2/0	**Happy Days**/*Hausmusik, Kinderpaar*	4¼″	OE
150/0	**Happy Days**/*Hausmusik, Kinderpaar*	5¼″	OE
150/I	**Happy Days**/*Hausmusik, Kinderpaar*	6¼″	OE
151/W	**Madonna**/*Sitzende Madonna mit sitzendem Kind*	12″	OE
151/11	**Madonna**/*Sitzende Madonna mit sitzendem Kind*	12″	OE

HUM No.	NAME	SIZE	STATUS
152/A/0	**Umbrella Boy**/*Geborgen, Junge*	4¾″	**OE**
152/A/II	**Umbrella Boy**/*Geborgen, Junge*	8″	**OE**
152/B/0	**Umbrella Girl**/*Geborgen, Mädchen*	4¾″	**OE**
152/B/II	**Umbrella Girl**/*Geborgen, Mädchen*	8″	**OE**
153/0	**Auf Wiedersehen**/*Auf Wiedersehen, Kinderpaar*	5″	**OE**
153/I	**Auf Wiedersehen**/*Auf Wiedersehen, Kinderpaar*	7″	**OE**
154/0	**Waiter**/*Herr Ober*	6″	**OE**
154/I	**Waiter**/*Herr Ober*	7″	**OE**
155			**CN**
156			**CN**
157			**CN**
158			**CN**
159			**CN**
160			**CN**
161			**CN**
162			**CN**
163	**Whitsuntide**/*Glockenturm mit Engeln*	7″	**OE**
164	**Holy Water Font**/*Am Wegesrand, Weihkessel*	2¾ x 4¾″	**OE**
165	**Swaying Lullaby**/*Kind mit Hängematte und Vögel, Wandring*	5¼ x 5¼″	**OE**
166	**Ashtray, Boy with bird**/*Ascher, Junge mit Vogel*	6 x 6¼″	**OE**
167	**Holy Water Font**/*Weihkessel, Sitzender Engel*	3 x 4¾″	**OE**
168	**Standing Boy, Plaque**/*Stehender Junge mit Herz und Flasche, Wandbild*	5¾ x 5¾″	**OE**
169	**Bird Duet**/*Frühlingslied*	4″	**OE**
170/I	**Schoolboys**/*Schweriges Problem*	7½″	**OE**
170/III	**Schoolboys**/*Schweriges Problem*	10¼″	**OE**
171	**Little Sweeper**/*Kehrliesl*	4¼″	**OE**
172/II	**Festival Harmony (Mandolin)**/*Adventsengel mit Mandoline*	10¼″	**OE**
172/0	**Festival Harmony (Mandolin)**/*Adventsengel mit Mandoline*	8″	**OE**
173/II	**Festival Harmony (Flute)**/*Adventsengel mit Flöte*	10¼″	**OE**
173/0	**Festival Harmony (Flute)**/*Adventsengel mit Flöte*	8″	**OE**
174	**She loves me, she loves me not!**/*Liebt mich, liebt mich nicht*	4¼″	**OE**
175	**Mother's Darling**/*Markt-Christel*	5½″	**OE**
176/0	**Happy Birthday**/*Gratulanten*	5½″	**OE**
176/I	**Happy Birthday**/*Gratulanten*	6″	**OE**
177/I	**Schoolgirls**/*s' Meisterstück*	7½″	**OE**
177/III	**Schoolgirls**/*s' Meisterstück*	9½″	**OE**
178	**The Photographer**/*Der Fotograf*	5¼″	**OE**
179	**Coquettes**/*Zaungäste*	5″	**OE**
180	**Tuneful Good Night**/*Wandschmuck in Herzform, sitzendes Kind mit Trompete*	5 x 4¾″	**OE**
181			**CN**
182	**Good Friends**/*Mädchen mit Böckchen*	4″	**OE**
183	**Forest Shrine**/*Waldandacht, Marterl*	9″	**OE**
184	**Latest News**/*Das Allerneueste*	5″	**OE**
185	**Accordion Boy**/*Bandoneonspieler*	5″	**OE**
186	**Sweet Music**/*Zum Tanz, Bassgeiger*	7″	**OE**
187	**M.I. Hummel Store Plaque (in English)**	5½ x 4″	**OE**
188	**Celestial Musician**/*Himmlische Klange*	7″	**OE**
189			**CN**
190			**CN**
191			**CN**
192	**Candlelight**/*Engel mit Kerze*	6¾″	**OE**
193	**Angel Duet**/*Stille Nacht, Engelgrüppchen*	5″	**OE**
194	**Watchful Angel**/*Schutzengel*	6¾″	**OE**
195/2/0	**Barnyard Hero**/*Angsthase*	4″	**OE**
195/I	**Barnyard Hero**/*Angsthase*	5½″	**OE**
196/0	**Telling Her Secret**/*Das Geheimnis*	5″	**OE**
196/I	**Telling Her Secret**/*Das Geheimnis*	6½″	**OE**
197/2/0	**Be Patient**/*Entenmütterchen*	4¼″	**OE**
197/I	**Be Patient**/*Entenmütterchen*	6¼″	**OE**
198/2/0	**Home from Market**/*Glückslauf, Junge mit Schweinchen im Korb*	4¼″	**OE**
198/I	**Home from Market**/*Glückslauf, Junge mit Schweinchen im Korb*	5½″	**OE**

HUM No.	NAME	SIZE	STATUS
199/0	**Feeding Time**/*Im Hühnerhof*	4¼″	**OE**
199/I	**Feeding Time**/*Im Hühnerhof*	5½″	**OE**
200/0	**Little Goat Herder**/*Ziegenbub*	4¾″	**OE**
200/I	**Little Goat Herder**/*Ziegenbub*	5½″	**OE**
201/2/0	**Retreat to Safety**/*In tausend Ängsten*	4″	**OE**
201/I	**Retreat to Safety**/*In tausend Ängsten*	5½″	**OE**
202			**CN**
203/2/0	**Signs of Spring**/*Frühlingsidyll*	4″	**OE**
203/I	**Signs of Spring**/*Frühlingsidyll*	5½″	**OE**
204	**Weary Wanderer**/*In Lauterbach hab i . . . ,*	6″	**OE**
205	**M.I. Hummel Store Plaque (in German)**	5½ x 4″	**CE**
206	**Holy Water Font, Angel Cloud**/*Weihkessel, Kind mit Blume*	2¼ x 4¾″	**OE**
207	**Holy Water Font**/*Weihkessel, Christkindlein kommt*	2 x 4¾″	**OE**
208	**M.I. Hummel Store Plaque (in French)**	5½ x 4″	**CE**
209	**M.I. Hummel Store Plaque (in Swedish)**	5½ x 4″	**CE**
210	**M.I. Hummel Store Plaque (in English)**	5½ x 4″	**CE**
211	**M.I. Hummel Store Plaque with Merry Wanderer**	5½ x 4″	**CE**
212			**CN**
213	**M.I. Hummel Store Plaque (in Spanish)**	5¼ x 4″	**CE**
214	**Nativity set with wooden stable**/*Krippensatz mit Holzstall*	6¼″	**OE**
214/A	**Virgin Mary**	6¼″	**OE**
214/A	**Infant Jesus**	1½ x 3½″	**OE**
214/B	**Joseph**	7½″	**OE**
214/C	**Angel, standing**	3½″	**OE**
214/D	**Angel, kneeling**	3″	**OE**
214/E	**We Congratulate**	3½″	**OE**
214/F	**Shepherd, standing**	7″	**OE**
214/G	**Shepherd, kneeling**	4¾″	**OE**
214/H	**Shepherd, kneeling with flute**	4″	**OE**
214/J	**Donkey**	5″	**OE**
214/K	**Ox**	3½ x 6¼″	**OE**
214/L	**Moorish King**	8¼″	**OE**
214/M	**King, kneeling**	5½″	**OE**
214/N	**King, kneeling, with cash-box**	5½″	**OE**
214/O	**Lamb**	1½ x 2″	**OE**
215			**CN**
216			**CN**
217	**Boy with Toothache**/*Schmerz lass nach*	5½″	**OE**
218/0	**Birthday Serenade**/*Geburtstagsständchen*	5¼″	**OE**
218/2/0	**Birthday Serenade**/*Geburtstagsständchen*	4¼″	**OE**
219			**CN**
220	**We Congratulate**/*Pärchen*	4″	**OE**
221			**CN**
222	**Madonna Plaque**/*Madonnenbild*	4 x 5″	**OE**
223	**Table Lamp, To Market**	9½″	**OE**
224/I	**Table Lamp, Wayside Harmony**	7½″	**OE**
224/II	**Table Lamp, Wayside Harmony**	9½″	**OE**
225/I	**Table Lamp, Just Resting**	7½″	**OE**
225/II	**Table Lamp, Just Resting**	9½″	**OE**
226	**The mail is here**/*Trara- die Post ist da*	4¼ x 6″	**OE**
227	**Table Lamp, She loves me, she loves me not . . .**	7½″	**OE**
228	**Table Lamp, Good Friends**	7½″	**OE**
229	**Table Lamp, Apple Tree Girl**	7½″	**OE**
230	**Table Lamp, Apple Tree Boy**	7½″	**OE**
231	**Table Lamp, Birthday Serenade**	9¾″	**OE**
232	**Table Lamp, Happy Days**	9¾″	**OE**
233			**CN**
234	**Table Lamp, Birthday Serenade**	7¾″	**OE**
235	**Table Lamp, Happy Days**	7¾″	**OE**
236			**CN**
237			**CN**
238/A	**Angel with lute**/*Engel mit Laute*	2″	**OE**
238/B	**Angel with accordion**/*Engel mit Bandoneon*	2″	**OE**

HUM No.	NAME	SIZE	STATUS
238/C	**Angel with trumpet**/*Engel mit Trompete*	2″	OE
239/A	**Girl with nosegay**/*Mädchen mit Blumenstrauss*	3½″	OE
239/B	**Girl with doll**/*Mädchen mit Puppe*	3½″	OE
239/C	**Boy with horse**/*Junge mit Holzpferd*	3½″	OE
240	**Little Drummer**/*Trommler*	4¼″	OE
241			CN
242			CN
243	**Holy Water Font, Madonna and Child**/*Weihkessel*	3 x 4″	OE
244			CN
245			CN
246	**Holy Water Font, Holy Family**/*Weihkessel, Heilige Familie*	3¼ x 4″	OE
247			CN
248	**Holy Water Font, Guardian Angel**/*Weihkessel*	2¼ x 5½″	OE
249			CN
250/A	**Goatherd, Book End**/*Ziegenbub, Buchstütze*	5½″	OE
250/B	**Feeding Time, Book End**/*Im Hühnerhof, Buchstütze*	5½″	OE
251/B	**She loves me, she loves me not!, Book End**/*Liebt mich, liebt mich nicht, Buchstütze*	5″	OE
251/A	**Good Friends, Book End**/*Freunde, Buchstütze*	5″	OE
252/B	**Apple Tree Boy, Book End**/*Herbst, Junge im Baum, Buchstütze*	5″	OE
252/A	**Apple Tree Girl, Book End**/*Frühling, Mädchen im Baum, Buchstütze*	5″	OE
253			CN
254			CN
255	**A stitch in time**/*Zwei rechts-zwei links*	6¾″	OE
256	**Knitting Lesson**/*Ob's gelingt?*	7½″	OE
257	**For Mother**/*Fürs Mütterchen*	5″	OE
258	**Which Hand?**/*Rat mal!*	5½″	OE
259			CN
260	**Large nativity set with wooden stable**/*Krippensatz, gross mit Holzstall*		OE
260/A	**Madonna**	9¾″	OE
260/B	**Saint Joseph**	11¾″	OE
260/C	**Infant Jesus**	5¾″	OE
260/D	**Good Night**	5¼″	OE
260/E	**Angel Serenade**	4¼″	OE
260/F	**We Congratulate**	6¼″	OE
260/G	**Shepherd, standing**	11¾″	OE
260/H	**Sheep standing with lamb**	3¾″	OE
260/J	**Shepherd Boy, kneeling**	7″	OE
260/K	**Little Tooter**	5⅛″	OE
260/L	**Donkey, standing**	7½″	OE
260/M	**Cow, lying**	6 x 11″	OE
260/N	**Moorish King, standing**	12¾″	OE
260/O	**King, standing**	12″	OE
260/P	**King, kneeling**	9″	OE
260/R	**One Sheep, lying**	3¼ x 4″	OE
261	**Angelic Song**/*Stille Nacht, ohne Kerzentülle*	5″	OE
262	**Heavenly Lullabye**	3½ x 5″	OE
263	**Merry Wanderer, Wall Plaque**	4 x 5¾″	CE
264	**Annual Plate, 1971, Heavenly Angel**/*Jahresteller, 1971*	7½″	CE
265	**Annual Plate, 1972, Hear Ye, Hear Ye**/*Jahresteller, 1972*	7½″	CE
266	**Annual Plate, 1973, Globetrotter**/*Jahresteller, 1973*	7½″	CE
267	**Annual Plate, 1974, Goose Girl**/*Jahresteller, 1974*	7½″	CE
268	**Annual Plate, 1975, Ride into Christmas**/*Jahresteller, 1975*	7½″	CE
269	**Annual Plate, 1976, Apple Tree Girl**/*Jahresteller, 1976*	7½″	OE
270	**Annual Plate, 1977, Apple Tree Boy**	7½″	ON
271			ON
272			ON
273			ON
274			ON
275			ON
276			ON
277			ON

HUM No.	NAME	SIZE	STATUS
278			ON
279			ON
280	**Anniversary Plate, 1975, Stormy Weather**	10″	CE
281			ON
282			ON
283			ON
284			ON
285			ON
286			ON
287			ON
288			ON
289			ON
290			ON
291			ON
292			ON
293			ON
294			ON
295			ON
296			ON
297			ON
298			ON
299			ON
300			ON
301			ON
302			ON
303			ON
304	**The Artist**/*Kunstmaler*	5½″	OE
305	**The Builder**/*Der Schwerarbeiter*	5½″	OE
306	**Little Bookkeeper**/*Stellvertretung*	4¾″	OE
307	**Good Hunting!**/*Weidmannsheil!*	5″	OE
308	**Little Tailor**/*Schneiderlein*	5½″	OE
309			ON
310			ON
311	**Kiss Me!**/*Hab'mich lieb!*	6″	OE
312			ON
313			ON
314	**Confidentially**/*Zweigespräch*	5½″	OE
315	**Mountaineer**/*I' hab's erreicht*	5″	OE
316			ON
317	**Not for you!**/*Nix für dich!*	6″	OE
318			ON
319	**Doll Bath**/*Puppenbad*	5″	OE
320			ON
321	**Wash Day**/*Grosse Wäsche*	6″	OE
322	**Little Pharmacist**/*Der Apotheker*	6″	OE
323			ON
324			ON
325			ON
326			ON
327	**The Run-a-way**/*Der frohe Wanderer*	5¼″	OE
328	**Carnival**/*Fastnach*	5¾″	OE
329			ON
330			ON
331	**Crossroads**/*Am Scheideweg*	6¾″	OE
332	**Soldier Boy**/*Stillgestanden!*	6″	OE
333	**Blessed Event**/*Das grosse Ereignis*	5½″	OE
334	**Homeward Bound**/*Heimkehr vom Felde*	5¼″	OE
335			ON
336	**Close Harmony**/*Geburtstagsständchen*	5½″	OE
337	**Cinderella**/*Aschenputtel*	4½″	OE
338			ON
339			ON

HUM No.	NAME	SIZE	STATUS
340	**Letter to Santa Claus**/*Brief an Christkind*	7¼''	OE
341			ON
342	**Mischief Maker**/*Der Störenfried*	5''	OE
344	**Feathered Friends**/*Schwanenteich*	4¾''	OE
345	**A Fair Measure**/*Der Kaufmann*	5½''	OE
346	**The Smart Little Sister**/*Das kluge Schwesterlein*	4¾''	OE
347	**Adventure Bound, The Seven Swabians**/*Die Sieben Schwaben*	7½ x 8¼''	OE
348	**Ring Around the Rosie**/*Ringelreihen*	6¾''	OE
349			ON
350			ON
351			ON
352			ON
353/0	**Spring Dance**/*Sommertanz*	5¼''	OE
353/I	**Spring Dance**/*Sommertanz*	6¾''	OE
354			CN
355	**Autumn Harvest**/*Herbstegen*	4¾''	OE
356	**Gay Adventure**/*Frohes Wandern*	5''	OE
357	**Guiding Angel**/*Kniender Engel mit Lanterne*	2¾''	OE
358	**Shining Light**/*Kniender Engel mit Kerze*	2¾''	OE
359	**Tuneful Angel**/*Kniender Engel mit Horn*	2¾''	OE
360/A	**Wall Vase, Boy and Girl**/*Wandvase, Junge und Mädchen*	4½ x 6¼''	OE
360/B	**Wall Vase, Boy**/*Wandvase, Junge*	4½ x 6¼''	OE
360/C	**Wall Vase, Girl**/*Wandvase, Mädchen*	4½ x 6¼''	OE
361	**Favorite Pet**/*Ostergruss*	4½''	OE
362			ON
363	**Big Housecleaning**/*Grossreinmachen*	4''	OE
364			ON
365			ON
366	**Flying Angel**/*Hängeengel*	3½''	OE
367	**Busy Student**/*Musterschülerin*	4¼''	OE
368			ON
369	**Follow the Leader**/*Mach mit*	7''	OE
370			ON
371			ON
372			ON
373			ON
374	**Lost Stocking**/*Hab mein Strumpf verloren*	4¼''	OE
375			ON
376			ON
377	**Bashful!**/*Vergissmeinnicht*	4¾''	OE
378	**Easter Greetings!**/*Ostergruss*	5¼''	OE
379			ON
380			ON
381	**Flower Vendor**/*Zum Blumenmarkt*	5¼''	OE
382	**Visiting an Invalid**/*Krankenbesuch*	5''	OE
383			ON
384	**Easter Time**/*Osterfreunde*	4''	OE
385	**Chicken-Licken!**/*Kükenliesl*	4¾''	OE
386	**On Secret Path**/*Auf heimlichen wegen*	5¼''	OE
387			ON
388	**Candlestick, Little Band**/*Leuchter Kindergruppe*	3 x 4¾''	OE
388/M	**Candlestick on Music Box, Little Band**/*Leuchter Kindergruppe auf Musikdose*	3 x 4¾''	OE
389	**Girl with sheet of music**/*Mädchen mit Notenblatt*	2¼''	OE
390	**Boy with accordion**/*Junge mit Bandoneon*	2¼''	OE
391	**Girl with trumpet**/*Mädchen mit Trompete*	2¼''	OE
392	**Group of Children**/*Kindergruppe*	3 x 4¾''	OE
392/M	**Group of Children on Music Box**/*Kindergruppe mit Musikwerk*	3 x 4¾''	OE
393			ON
394			ON
395			ON
396	**Ride into Christmas**/*Fahrt in die Weihnacht*	5¾''	OE

"Puppy Love"
"Geigerlein" mit Hund
> **HUM 1 .... 5"**

"Little Fiddler"
"Geigerlein" ohne Hund
> **HUM 2/0........ 6"**
> **2/I........ 7½"**
> **2/II....... 10¾"**
> **2/III...... 12¼"**

Same as HUM 4 except it has brown hat. Called "Violinist" in old catalogs. Known size variations.

"Book Worm"
"Der Bücherwurm"
> **HUM 3/I........ 5½"**
> **3/II....... 8"**
> **3/III...... 9"**

Is known to have appeared in size 3/II (8") but with arabic 2 size designator (3/2).

"Little Fiddler"
"Geigerlein" ohne Hund
> **HUM 4 .... 4¾"**

Same as HUM 2 except it has black hat. Known color variations. Known size variations.

HUM 1   "Puppy Love"

HUM 2 "Little Fiddler"

HUM 4 "Little Fiddler"

HUM 3 "Book Worm"

"Strolling Along"
"Wanderbub" mit Hund
     HUM 5 .... 4¾"
Older models have eyes which glance off to one side. Newer models look straight on. Known variations in brown color of dog.

"Sensitive Hunter"
"Jägerlein"
     HUM 6/0........ 4¾"
        6/I........ 5½"
        6/II....... 7½"
Lederhosen straps appear either parallel or crossed.

"Merry Wanderer"
"Wanderbub" ohne Hund
     HUM 7/0........ 6¼"
        7/I........ 7"
        7/II....... 9½"
        7/III...... 11¼"
Several known size variations.

"Book Worm"
"Der Bücherwurm"
     HUM 8 .... 4"
Same as HUM 3 except smaller size.

HUM 5 "Strolling Along"

HUM 6 "Sensitive Hunter"

HUM 7 "Merry Wanderer"

HUM 8 "Book Worm"

"Begging his Share"
"Gratulant"
> **HUM 9 .... 5½"**

Appears with candleholder and without. Known size variations.

Flower Madonna
Blumen-Madonna mit Kind
> **HUM 10/I/W... 8¼"**
> **10/I/11 .. 8¼"**
> **10/III/W.11½"**
> **10/III/11.11½"**

Older models have "donut hole" halo. New halo is "full cap." Known size variations. Also manufactured in glazed white.

HUM 9 "Begging his Share"

HUM 10   Flower Madonna

Merry Wanderer
Wanderbub ohne Hund
> **HUM 11/2/0.... 4¼″**
> **11/0 ...... 4¾″**

Same as HUM 7

Chimney Sweep
"Ich bringe Glück",
Kaminfeger
> **HUM 12/2/0.... 4″**
> **12/I....... 5½″**

Known size variations.

Meditation
Die Gratulantin
> **HUM 13/2/0.... 4¼″**
> **13/0 ...... 5½″**
> **13/II ..... 7″**
> **13/V...... 13¾″**

Is known to have appeared in size 13/II (7″) but with arabic 2 size designator. Flowers in half of basket on 13/II. Flowers in all of basket on 13/V.

HUM 11   Merry Wanderer

HUM 12   Chimney Sweep

HUM 13   Meditation

Book Worm, Book Ends, Boy and Girl
Der Bücherwurm, Buchstütze Junge und Mädchen
HUM 14/A&B..5½″
Holes for sand to weight book ends in bottom of older models, sealed with small pieces of cork.

HUM 14/A&B   Book Worm, Book Ends, Boy and Girl

Hear Ye, Hear Ye
"Hört Ihr Leute",
Nachtwächter
> **HUM 15/0 ......5″**
> **15/I.......6″**
> **15/II .....7″**

Little Hiker
Hans im Glück
> **HUM 16/2/0.... 4½″**
> **16/I.......6″**

Congratulations
Ich gratuliere
> **HUM 17.........6″**

Is known to have appeared in 17/0 size, and also at 8″ but marked with 17_2 size designator. Recent models have socks and a new hairstyle.

Christ Child
Stille Nacht, Jesuskind
> **HUM 18.........2x6″**

Is known to have appeared in white overglaze (rare).

HUM 15 Hear Ye, Hear Ye

HUM 16   Little Hiker

HUM 17   Congratulations

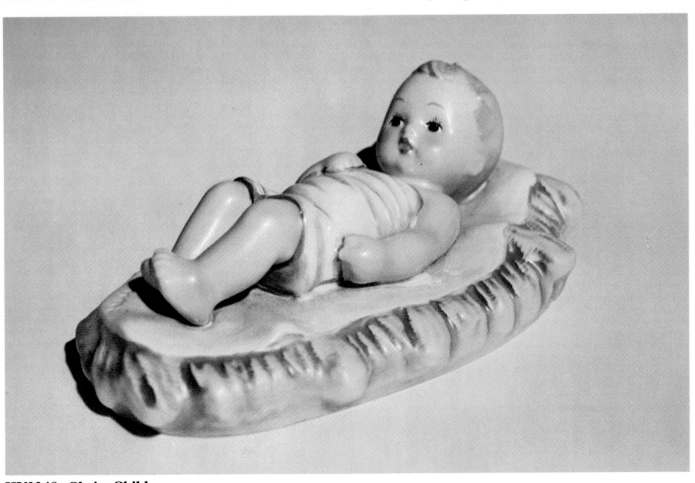

HUM 18   Christ Child

Prayer before Battle
Der fromme Reitersmann
> HUM 20 . . . . 4¼″

Heavenly Angel
Christkindlein kommt, Engel
> HUM 21/0 . . . . . . 4¾″
> 21/0/½ . . . 6¾″
> 21/II . . . . . 8¾″

Only figurine to have "½" size designator. Many known size variations.

Holy Water Font, Sitting Angel
Weihkessel, sitzender Engel
> HUM 22/0 . . . . 2¾x3½″
> 22/I . . . . 3¼x4″

Variations of color and bowl design known to exist.

HUM 20 Prayer before Battle

HUM 21 Heavenly Angel

HUM 22 Holy Water Font, Sitting Angel

Adoration
Bei Mutter Maria, Marterl
> **HUM 23/I** . . . . 6¼″
> **23/III** . . . . 9″

Known to have appeared in white overglaze (rare).

Lullaby
Wiegenlied
> **HUM 24/I** . . . . 3½x5″
> **24/III** . . . . 6x8″

HUM 24/III is considered rare. Variations occur in style of candleholder.

HUM 23 Adoration

Angelic Sleep
Stille Nacht
> **HUM 25** . . . . **3½x5″**

Known to have appeared in white overglaze.

Holy Water Font, Child Jesus
Weihkessel,
> **HUM 26/I** . . . . . . **2½x6″**
> **26/0** . . . . . . **1½x5″**

Joyous News
O, du fröliche
> **HUM 27/III** . . . . **4¼x4¾″**

Known to have appeared in 27/III size with arabic 3 size designator. Similar in appearance to 238/C. Considered to be rare.

Wayside Devotion
Abendlied, Marterl
> **HUM 28/II** . . . . . **7½″**
> **28/III** . . . . **8¾″**

Known to have appeared in 28/II size but with arabic 2 size designator (7½″).

HUM 25   Angelic Sleep

HUM 26　Holy Water Font, Child Jesus

HUM 28　Wayside Devotion

HUM 27　Joyous News

Holy Water Font, Guardian Angel

Weihkessel

HUM 29 .... 2½x5¾″
29/0 ...... 2⅜x6″

Fragile wings. Redesigned into HUM 248.

Ba-Bee Ring

Hui, die Hummel, Wandring

HUM 30A&B ... 4¾x5″

Is known to have appeared in 30/I size.

Advent Group with Candle (CE)

Adventsgruppe mit kerzen

HUM 31 ....

Little Gabriel

O, du fröhliche . . . , Engel

HUM 32/0 ...... 5″

Known size variations.

HUM 29   Holy Water Font, Guardian Angel

HUM 30A&B   Ba-Bee Ring

HUM 32 Little Gabriel

Ashtray, Joyful
Gesangsprobe, Ascher
        HUM 33.........3½x6″

Ashtray, Singing Lesson
's stimmt net, Ascher
        HUM 34.........3½x6¼″

Holy Water Font, The Good Shepherd
Der gute Hirte, Weihkessel
        HUM 35/0 ......2¼x4¾″
        35/I.......2¾x5¾″

Holy Water Font
Weihkessel, sitzender Engel
        HUM 36/0 ......2¾x4″
        36/I.......3½x4½″

HUM 33 Ashtray, Joyful

HUM 34 Ashtray, Singing Lesson

HUM 36　Holy Water Font

HUM 35　Holy Water Font, The Good Shepherd

Herald Angels, Candlestick
Adventsleuchter mit 3 Engeln
>HUM 37.........2½x4″

**Angel, Joyous News with
Lute, Candleholder**
Adventsengelchen mit Laute
>HUM I/38/0....2″
>III/38/0..2″
>III/38/I..2¾″

Roman numerals to the left of
the **HUM** number indicate the
size of the candle that fits into
the figurine. Size I is .6 cm, size
III is 1 cm. (Note: Not all
figurines which hold candles are
photographed with candles in
this book, but they are always
sold with candles.)

**Angel, Joyous News, with
Accordion, Candleholder**
*Adventsengelchen mit
Bandoneon*
>HUM I/39/0....2″
>III/39/0..2″
>III/39/I..2¾″

Roman numerals to the left of
the **HUM** number indicate the
size of the candle that fits into
the figurine. Size I is .6 cm, size
III is 1 cm. (Note: Not all
figurines which hold candles are
photographed with candles in
this book, but they are always
sold with candles.)

**Angel, Joyous News, with
Trumpet, Candleholder**
Adventsengelchen mit Trompete
>HUM I/40/0....2″
>III/40/0..2″
>III/40/I..2¾″

Roman numerals to the left of
the **HUM** number indicate the
size of the candle that fits into
the figurine. Size I is .6 cm, size
III is 1 cm. (Note: Not all
figurines which hold candles are
photographed with candles in
this book, but they are always
sold with candles.)

Good Shepherd
Der gute Hirte
>HUM 42.........6¼″

HUM 37   Herald Angels, Candlestick

HUM 38 Angel, Joyous News with Lute, Candleholder;   39 with Accordion, Candleholder; 40 with Trumpet, Candleholder.

HUM 42 Good Shepherd

March Winds
Lausbub
  HUM 43.........5″
Known to have been redesigned.

Culprits
Table Lamp
  HUM 44A.......8½″

Out of Danger
Table Lamp
  HUM 44B.......8½″

HUM 43   March Winds

HUM 44A   Culprits   **44B   Out of Danger**

Madonna with halo
Madonna mit Heiligenschein

HUM 45/0/W .. 10½″
45/0/6.... 10½″
45/0/13 .. 10½″
45/I/W... 12″
45/I/6.... 12″
45/I/13... 12″
45/III/W 16¾″
45/III/6.. 16¾″
45/III/13 16¾″

Has also appeared in white overglaze.

Madonna without halo
Madonna ohne Heiligenschein

HUM 46/0/W .. 10¼″
46/0/6.... 10¼″
46/0/13 .. 10¼″
46/I/W... 11¼″
46/I/6.... 11¼″
46/I/13... 11¼″
46/III/W 16¼″
46/III/6.. 16¼″
46/III/13 16¼″

Has also appeared in white overglaze.

HUM 45   Madonna with halo

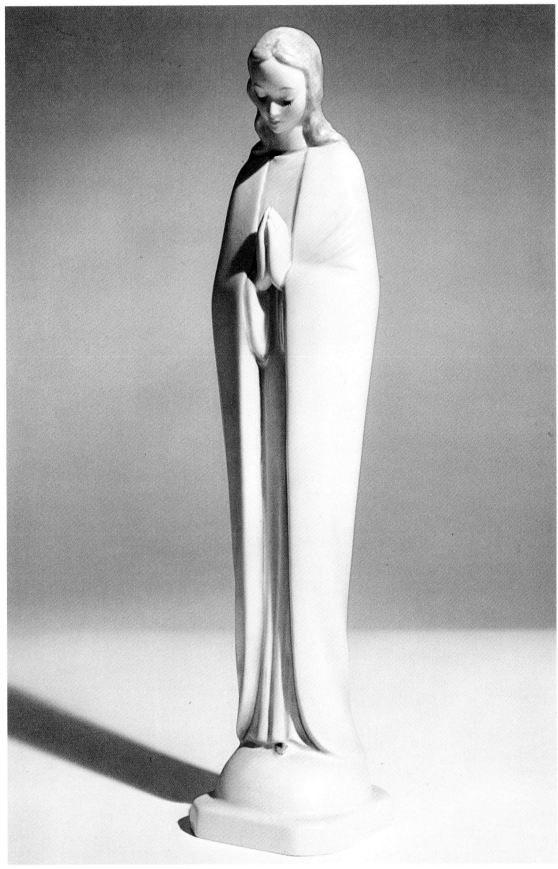

HUM 46 Madonna without halo

Goose Girl
Gänseliesl
> **HUM 47/3/0.... 4"**
> **47/0 ...... 4¾"**
> **47/II ..... 7½"**

Is known to have appeared in 47/II size but with arabic 2 designator (7½").

Madonna Plaque
Madonnen-Bild
> **HUM 48/0 ...... 3x4"**
> **48/II ..... 4¾x6"**

Is known to have appeared in white overglaze and bisque (rare). Has appeared in 48/V size but with arabic 5 designator (8¼x10½").

To Market
Brüderlein und Schwesterlein
> **HUM 49/3/0.... 4"**
> **49/0 ...... 5½"**
> **49/I....... 6¼"**

Is known to have been produced in 49/0 size but with decimal point after "49" to indicate "0" size (49.).

Volunteers
Soldatenspiel
> **HUM 50/2/0.... 5"**
> **50/0 ...... 5½"**
> **50/I....... 6½"**

Known size variations.

HUM 47 Goose Girl

HUM 49 To Market

HUM 48 Madonna Plaque

HUM 50 Volunteers

Village Boy
Dorfbub
>   **HUM 51/3/0.... 4″**
>   **51/2/0.... 5″**
>   **51/0 ...... 6″**
>   **51/I....... 7¼″**

Going to Grandma's
Hausmütterchen
>   **HUM 52/0 ...... 4¾″**
>   **52/I....... 6″**

Has been produced with both oval and rectangular bases.

Joyful
Gesangsprobe
>   **HUM 53 .... 4″**

Known size variations.

Joyful, Box
Gesangsprobe, Dose
>   **HUM III/53 .... 6″**

Older models have lid top. Newer models have jar top.

HUM 51 Village Boy

HUM 52 Going to Grandma's

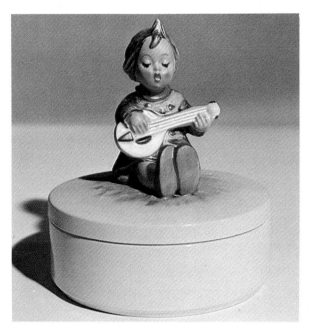

HUM III/53 Joyful, Box

HUM 53 Joyful

Silent Night
Stille Nacht, Krippe
 HUM 54.........5½x4¾"
Rare variation with black boy in
crib scene.

Saint George
Ritter Heilige Georg
 HUM 55.........6¾"

Culprits
Apfeldieb, Junge
 HUM 56/A......6¼"

Out of Danger
In Sicherheit, Mädchen
 HUM 56/B......6¼"

HUM 54   Silent Night

HUM 55   Saint George

HUM 56/A   Culprits

56/B   Out of Danger

Chick Girl
Kückenmütterchen

> **HUM 57/0 ......3½″**
> **57/I.......4¼″**

Small size has two chicks. Large size has three chicks.

Chick Girl, box
Kückenmütterchen, Dose

> **HUM III/57 ....6¼″**

Older models have lid top. Newer models have jar top.

Playmates
Hasenvater

> **HUM 58/0 ......4″**
> **58/I.......4¼″**

Skier
Ski-heil

> **HUM 59 ....5″**

Known size variations.

HUM 57 Chick Girl

HUM III/57 Chick Girl, box

HUM 58   Playmates

HUM 59   Skier

HUM III/58 Playmates, box

Book Ends: Farm Boy
Schweinhirt, Buchstützen
      HUM 60/A......4¾″

Book Ends: Goose Girl
Gänseliesl, Buchstützen
      HUM 60/B......4¾″

Book Ends: Playmates
Hasenvater, Buchstützen
      HUM 61/A......4″

Book Ends: Chick Girl
Kückenmütterchen, Buchstützen
      HUM 61/B......4″

Happy Pastime, Ashtray
Strickliesl, Ascher
      HUM 62.........3½x6¼″

Singing lesson
's stimmt net
      HUM 63.........2¾″

Singing lesson, box
's stimmt net, Dose
      HUM III/63 .... 6″
Older models have lid top.
Newer models have jar top.

HUM 60/B Book Ends: Goose Girl   Book Ends: Farm Boy 60/A

HUM 61/A Book Ends: Playmates   Book Ends: Chick Girl 61/B

HUM 62   Happy Pastime, Ashtray

HUM 63   Singing lesson

HUM III/63   Singing lesson, box

Shepherd's Boy
Schäferbub
  HUM 64.........5½"
Known size variations.

Farewell
Auf Wiedersehen
  HUM 65.........4¾"
Known size variations "Decimal point" (65.) indicated "I" size (5").

Farm Boy
Schweinhirt
  HUM 66.........5"
Known size variations.

Doll Mother
Puppenmütterchen
  HUM 67.........4¾"
Known size variations.

HUM 64 Shepherd's Boy

HUM 65 Farewell

HUM 67 Doll Mother

HUM 66 Farm Boy

Lost Sheep
Schäferbub
> **HUM 68/2/0....** 4¼″
> **68/0 ......** 5½″

Known size variations.

Happy Pastime
Strickliesl
> **HUM 69........** 3½″

Happy Pastime, box
Strickliesl, Dose
> **HUM III/69 ....** 6″

Older models have lid top.
Newer models have jar top.

The Holy Child
Jesulein
> **HUM 70........** 6¾″

Known size variations.

HUM 68   Lost Sheep

HUM 69   Happy Pastime

HUM III/69   Happy Pastime, box

HUM 70   The Holy Child

Stormy Weather
Unter einem Dach
     HUM 71 . . . . 6¼″
Known size variations.

Spring Cheer
Frühling ist's
     HUM 72 . . . . 5″
Known color variations in dress.

Little Helper
Fleissiges Lieschen
     HUM 73 . . . . 4″

HUM 71 Stormy Weather

HUM 72 Spring Cheer   **HUM 73 Little Helper**

Little Gardener
Die kleine Gärtnerin
> **HUM 74.........4″**

Has been produced with both oval and round bases.

Holy Water Font, White Angel
Weihkessel, Weisser Engel
> **HUM 75.........1¾x3½″**

Book Ends, Doll Mother & Prayer before Battle
> **HUM 76A&B...(CE)**

Infant of Krumbad
Jesuskind, liegend
> **HUM**
> > 78/VIII/83 . 13¼″
> > 78/VI/83....10″
> > 78/V/83.....7¾″
> > 78/III/83 ...5½″
> > 78/II/83 ....3½″
> > 78/I/83......2½″
> > 78/VIII/11 .13½″
> > 78/VI/11....10″
> > 78/V/11.....7¾″
> > 78/III/11 ...5¼″
> > 78/II/11 ....3½″
> > 78/I/11......2½″
> > 78/0 ....2¼″

Has appeared in flesh and bisque.

Globe Trotter
Hinaus in die Ferne
> **HUM 79.........5″**

Design of basket weave is known to vary.

HUM 74 Little Gardener

HUM 75 Holy Water Font, White Angel

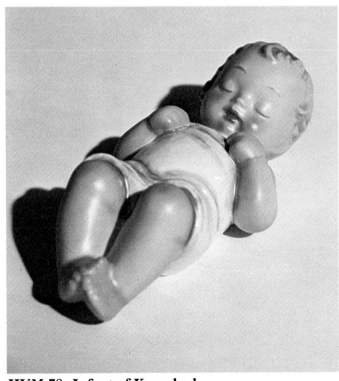

HUM 78 Infant of Krumbad

HUM 79 Globe Trotter

Little Scholar
Erster Schulgang, Junge
>   HUM 80 . . . . 5½″

School girl
Erster Schulgang, Mädchen
>   HUM 81/2/0 . . . . 4¼″
>   81/0 . . . . . . 5″

Known to have been manufactured in 81/0 size but with
"decimal point" to designate
"0" size designator (81.).

School Boy
Schulschwänzer, Junge
>   HUM 82/2/0 . . . . 4″
>   82/0 . . . . . . 5″
>   82/II . . . . . 7½″

Known size variations.

Angel Serenade
Fromme Weisen
>   HUM 83 . . . . 5½″

Very rare.

HUM 80 Little Scholar

HUM 81 School girl

94

HUM 82 School Boy

HUM 83 Angel Serenade

Worship
Am Wegesrand, Bildstöckl
> **HUM 84/0 ...... 5"**
> **84/V ...... 12¾"**

Known to have been manufactured in 84/V size but with arabic 5 designator.

Serenade
Ständchen, Junge mit Flöte
> **HUM 85/0 ...... 4¾"**
> **85/II ..... 7½"**

Known to have been produced in II size but with arabic 2 designator (7½").

Happiness
Wanderlied, Mädchen
> **HUM 86 .... 4¾"**

HUM 84 Worship

HUM 86 Happiness

HUM 85 Serenade

For Father
Fürs Vaterle, Rettichbub
   HUM 87.........5½″

Heavenly Protection
Schutzenengel
   HUM 88/II .....9″
      88/I.......6¾″
Known color variations.

HUM 87 For Father

HUM 88
Heavenly Protection

Little Cellist
Heimkehr, Bassgeiger
> **HUM 89/I.......6″**
> **89/II .....7½″**

Known variations with open and closed eyes.

Book Ends (CE)
Wayside Devotion &
Adoration
> **HUM 90A&B...**

Holy Water Font, Angel looking left
Weihkessel, Engel links schauend
> **HUM 91/A......2x4¾″**

Holy Water Font, Angel looking right
Weihkessel, Engel rechts schauend
> **HUM 91/B......2x4¾″**

Variations with and without halos.

HUM 89 Little Cellist

HUM 91/B Holy Water Font, Angel looking right   **HUM 91/A Holy Water Font, Angel looking left**

Merry Wanderer, Plaque
Wanderbub, Wandbild
      HUM 92.........5x5½″

Little Fiddler, Plaque
Geigerlein, Wandbild
      HUM 93.........5x5½″

Surprise
Hänsel und Gretel
      HUM 94/3/0....4″
      94/I......5½″

Brother
Dorfheld
      HUM 95.........5½″

Little Shopper
Gretel
      HUM 96.........4¾″
Known size variations.

Trumpet Boy
Der kleine Musikant
      HUM 97.........4¾″

HUM 92 Merry Wanderer, Plaque

HUM 93 Little Fiddler, Plaque

HUM 94 Surprise

HUM 96 Little Shopper

HUM 95 Brother

HUM 97 Trumpet Boy

Sister
Der erste Einkauf
    HUM 98/2/0.... 4¾″
        98/0 ...... 5½″
Known size variations.

Eventide
Abendlied
    HUM 99 .... 4¼x4¾″

Shrine—table lamp (CE)
Marterl—Lampenfuss mit Figur
    HUM 100........ 7½″
Very rare.

HUM 98   Sister

HUM 99 Eventide

HUM 100 Shrine—table lamp

Table Lamp—To Market (CE)
    HUM 101........

Table Lamp—Volunteers (CE)
    HUM 102

Table Lamp—Farewell (CE)
    HUM 103

Table Lamp—Wayside Devotion (CE)
    HUM 104

Plaque—Merry Wanderer (CE)
    HUM 106

Plaque—Little Fiddler (CE)
    HUM 107

Happy Traveller
Hinaus in die Ferne
    HUM 109/0 ..... 5″
    109/II .... 7½″

Let's Sing
Heini, Bandoneonspieler
    HUM 110/0 ..... 3″
    110/I ..... 4″

Let's Sing, box
    HUM III/110 ... 6″
Older models have lid tops. Newer models have jar tops.

Wayside Harmony
Vaters G'scheitester
    HUM 111/3/0 .. 4″
    111/1 ..... 5″
Known size variations.

Just Resting
Mutters Liebste
    HUM 112/3/0 .. 4″
    112/I ..... 5″
Known size variations.

HUM 109 Happy Traveller

HUM 110   Let's Sing

HUM 111   Wayside Harmony

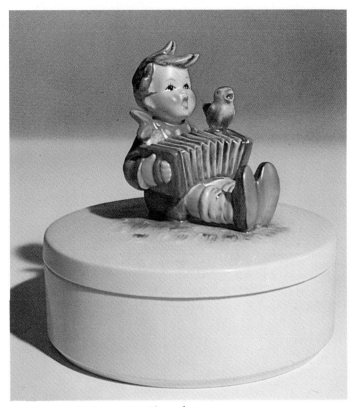

HUM III/110   Let's Sing, box

HUM 112   Just Resting

Heavenly Song
Stille Nacht, Adventsgruppe
> **HUM 113........3½x4¾″**

Let's Sing, Ashtray
Heini, Ascher
> **HUM 114........3½x6¼″**

Two variations, left and right. Older models have accordion player on right.

Advent candlestick: Girl with nosegay
Adventsleuchter: Mädchen mit Blumenstrauss
> **HUM 115........3½″**

Advent candlestick: Girl with fir tree
Adventsluechter: Mädchen mit Tannenbaum
> **HUM 116........3½″**

Advent candlestick: Boy with horse
Adventsleuchter: Junge mit Holzpferd
> **HUM 117........3½″**

HUM 113   Heavenly Song

HUM 114   Let's Sing, Ashtray

HUM 117 Advent candlestick: Boy with horse   HUM 116   Girl with fir tree   HUM 115   Girl with nosegay

Little Thrifty
Spar-Hummelchen
        HUM 118........5″
Known base design changes.

Postman
Eilbote
        HUM 119........5″
Known size variations.

Joyful and Let's Sing (CE)
(on wooden base)
        HUM 120........

Wayside Harmony and Just Resting (CE)
(on wooden base)
        HUM 121........

Puppy Love, Serenade and Happiness (CE)
(on wooden base)
        HUM 122........

Max and Moritz
Max und Moritz
        HUM 123........5″
Known size variations

Chef, Hello
        HUM 124/0.....6¼″
        124/I.....7″
Known size variations.
Known color variations.

HUM 118   Little Thrifty

HUM 119   Postman

HUM 124   Chef, Hello

HUM 123   Max and Moritz

Vacation-Time, plaque
Ferienfreunde, Bild
> HUM 125........ 4x4¾"

Retreat to Safety, plaque
Angsthase, Bild
> HUM 126........ 4¾x4¾"

Doctor
Puppendoktor
> HUM 127........ 4¾"

Baker
Der kleine Konditor
> HUM 128........ 4¾"

HUM 125   Vacation-Time, plaque

HUM 126   Retreat to Safety, plaque

HUM 127   Doctor

HUM 128   Baker

Band Leader
Herr Kappellmeister
>   HUM 129........5″

Duet
Duett, Sängerpaar
>   HUM 130........5″
Known size variations.

Street Singer
Kammersänger
>   HUM 131........5″

Star Gazer
Sterngucker
>   HUM 132........4¾″
Older models have blue shirt. Newer models have purple shirt.

Mother's Helper
Mutters Stütze
>   HUM 133........5″
Known size variations.

HUM 129 Band Leader

HUM 130 Duet

HUM 132 Star Gazer

HUM 131 Street Singer

HUM 133 Mother's Helper

Plaque "Quartet"
Bild "Das Quartett"
　　　HUM 134........ 6 x 6"

Soloist
Heldentenor
　　　HUM 135........ 4¾"

Friends
Gute Freunde
　　　HUM 136/I ..... 5"
　　　136/V .... 10¾"

Wall Plaque, Child in Bed
Wandring, Kind im Bettchen
　　　HUM 137........ 2¾x2¾"
Has appeared with HUM
137/A and 137/B incised on
bottom of base.

Flitting Butterfly
*Sitzendes Kind mit
Schmetterling, Wandring*
　　　HUM 139........ 2½x2½"

HUM 134　Plaque "Quartet"

HUM 135   Soloist

HUM 137   Wall Plaque, Child in Bed

HUM 136   Friends

HUM 139   Flitting Butterfly

The mail is here, plaque
Trara—die Post ist da, Bild
   HUM 140........ 4¼x6¼″

Apple Tree Girl
Frühling, Mädchen im Baum
   HUM 141/3/0 .. 4″
   141/I ..... 6″
   141/V .... 10″
   141/X .... 28″
Known base variations. Known size variations. Known as "Spring" in older catalogs.

Apple Tree Boy
Herbst, Junge im Baum
   HUM 142/3/0 .. 4″
   142/I ..... 6″
   142/V .... 10″
   142/X .... 28″
Known size variations. Known base variations. Known as "Fall" in older catalogs.

HUM 140 The mail is here, plaque

HUM 142 Apple Tree Boy   **HUM 141 Apple Tree Girl**

Boots
Meister Wichtig
     HUM 143/0 ..... 5½″
       143/I ..... 6½″

Angelic Song
Singendes Kind mit Engelein
     HUM 144....... 4″

"Little Guardian"
Betendes Kind mit Engelein
     HUM 145....... 4″

HUM 143　Boots

HUM 144　Angelic Song

HUM 145 "Little Guardian"

**Holy Water Font, Angel
Duet**
Weihkessel, Engelgrüppchen
     HUM 146........3¼x4¼"

**Holy Water Font, Angel
Shrine**
Weihkessel, Engel
     HUM 147........3x5"
Formerly named Angel Devo-
tion in old catalogs.

Happy Days
Hausmusik, Kinderpaar
     HUM 150/2/0..4¼"
        150/0.....5¼"
        150/I.....6¼"

Madonna
*Sitzende Madonna mit
sitzendem Kind*
     HUM 151/W....12"
        151/11....12"
Is known to have been produced
in white overglaze. Also produced in color with blue cloak.
Blue cloaked Madonna considered extremely rare.

HUM 146 Holy Water Font, Angel Duet

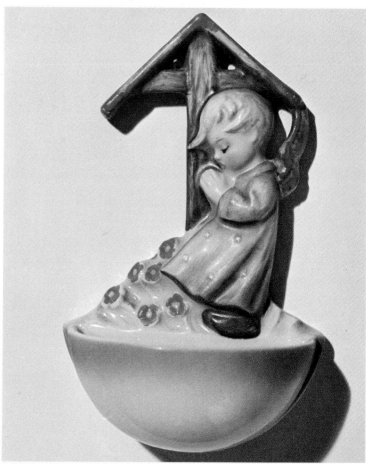

HUM 147 Holy Water Font, Angel Shrine

HUM 150   Happy Days

HUM 151   Madonna

Umbrella Boy
Geborgen, Junge
   HUM 152/A/0 .... 4¾″
        152/A/II ... 8″

Umbrella Girl
Geborgen, Mädchen
   HUM 152/B/0 .... 4¾″
        152/B/II ... 8″

HUM 152A Umbrella Boy

HUM 152B Umbrella Girl

Auf Wiedersehen

Auf Wiedersehen, Kinderpaar
> **HUM 153/0 ..... 5″**
> **153/I ..... 7″**

Known to have been produced with boy wearing cap. Variation considered extremely rare.

Waiter

Herr Ober
> **HUM 154/0 ..... 6″**
> **154/I ..... 7″**

Has been produced with various names on wine bottle. Older models have darker trousers.

Whitsuntide

Glockenturm mit Engeln
> **HUM 163 .... 7″**

Very rare. Known size variations.

Holy Water Font

Am Wegesrand, Weihkessel
> **HUM 164 .... 2¾x4¾″**

Swaying Lullabye

Kind mit Hängematte und Vögel, Wandring
> **HUM 165 .... 5¼x5¼″**

HUM 153 Auf Wiedersehen

HUM 154 Waiter

HUM 163   Whitsuntide

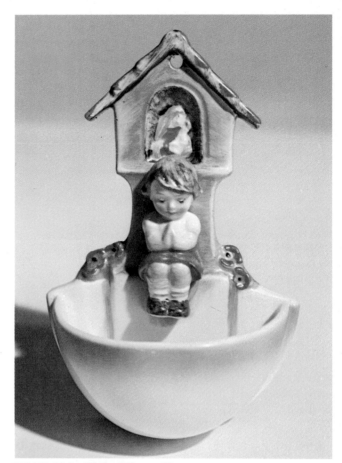

HUM 164   Holy Water Font

HUM 165   Swaying Lullabye

Ashtray, Boy with bird
Ascher, Junge mit Vogel
> **HUM 166........6x6¼″**

Holy Water Font
Weihkessel, Sitzender Engel
> **HUM 167........3x4¾″**

Standing Boy, Plaque
Stehender Junge mit Herz und
Flasche, Wandbild
> **HUM 168........5¾x5¾″**

Bird Duet
Frühlingslied
> **HUM 169........4″**

HUM 166   Ashtray, Boy with bird

HUM 167   Holy Water Font

HUM 168 Standing Boy, Plaque

HUM 169 Bird Duet

Schoolboys
Schweriges Problem
> **HUM 170/I ..... 7½"**
> **170/III ... 10¼"**

Little Sweeper
Kehrliesl
> **HUM 171........ 4¼"**

Festival Harmony (Mandolin)
Adventsengel mit Mandoline
> **HUM 172/II .... 10¼"**
> **172/0 ..... 8"**

On older models flowers grew up the figurine, with a bird on top of the flowers. Newer model finds bird on mandolin, flowers at feet. See variations.

Festival Harmony (Flute)
Adventsengel mit Flöte
> **HUM 173/II .... 10¼"**
> **173/0 ..... 8"**

On older models flowers grew up the figurine. Bird was larger. Newer model finds bird on arm, small flowers at feet.
See variations.

She loves me, she loves me not!
Liebt mich, liebt mich nicht
> **HUM 174........ 4¼"**

HUM 170   Schoolboys

HUM 171 Little Sweeper

HUM 173 Festival Harmony (Flute)

HUM 172 Festival Harmony (Mandolin)

HUM 174 She loves me, she loves me not!

Mother's Darling
Markt-Christel
> **HUM 175........5½″**

Happy Birthday
Gratulanten
> **HUM 176/0.....5½″**
> **176/I.....6″**

Has appeared in 176/0 size but
with "decimal point" (176.) size
designator (5½″).

Schoolgirls
s' Meisterstück
> **HUM 177/I.....7½″**
> **177/III...9½″**

HUM 175   Mother's Darling

HUM 176   Happy Birthday

HUM 177   Schoolgirls

The Photographer
Der Fotograf
HUM 178........5¼"

Coquettes
Zaungäste
HUM 179........5"

Tuneful Good Night
Wandschmuck in Herzform,
sitzendes Kind mit Trompete
HUM 180........5x4¾"
Considered rare.

Good Friends
Mädchen mit Böckchen
HUM 182........4"

Forest Shrine
Waldandacht, Marterl
HUM 183........9"
Considered very rare.

Latest News
Das Allerneueste
HUM 184........5"
Several variations in name of newspaper. Base variations. Variations in face of reader.

HUM 178   The Photographer

HUM 179   Coquettes

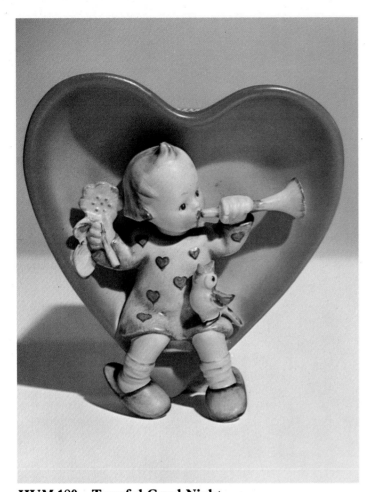

HUM 180   Tuneful Good Night

HUM 183   Forest Shrine

HUM 182   Good Friends

HUM 184   Latest News

Accordion Boy
Bandoneonspieler
      HUM 185........5″
Known size variations.

Sweet Music
Zum Tanz, Bassgeiger
      HUM 186........7″

M.I. Hummel
Store Plaque (in English)
      HUM 187........5½x4″
Redesigned from older style.
See chapter on variations.

Celestial Musician
Himmlische Klange
      HUM 188........7″

HUM 185 Accordion Boy

HUM 186 Sweet Music

HUM 187 M.I. Hummel Store Plaque (in English)

HUM 188 Celestial Musician

Candlelight
Engel mit Kerze
    HUM 192........ 6¾″
Produced with long and short candles.

Angel Duet
Stille Nacht, Engelgrüppchen
    HUM 193........5″
Similar to HUM 261.

Watchful Angel
Schutzengel
    HUM 194........6¾″
Called "Angelic Care" in old catalogs.

HUM 192   Candlelight

UM 193   Angel Duet

HUM 194   Watchful Angel

Barnyard Hero
Angsthase
> **HUM 195/2/0 .. 4″**
> **195/I ..... 5½″**

Telling her secret
Das Geheimnis
> **HUM 196/0 ..... 5″**
> **196/I ..... 6½″**

Known to have been produced in HUM 196/0 size but with decimal point (196.) size designator (5″).

Be Patient
Entenmütterchen
> **HUM 197/2/0 .. 4¼″**
> **197/I ..... 6¼″**

Known to have been produced in HUM 197/I size but with decimal point (197.) size indicator (6¼″).

Home from Market
Glückslauf, Junge mit
Schweinchen im Korb
> **HUM 198/2/0 .. 4¼″**
> **198/I ..... 5½″**

Known to have been produced in HUM 198/I size but with decimal point (198.) size indicator (5½″).

Feeding Time
Im Hühnerhof
> **HUM 199/0 ..... 4¼″**
> **199/I ..... 5½″**

Known to have been produced in HUM 199/I size but with decimal point (199.) size indicator (5½″).

HUM 195 Barnyard Hero

HUM 196 Telling her secret

HUM 197 Be Patient

HUM 199   Feeding Time

HUM 198   Home from Market

Little Goat Herder
Ziegenbub
> **HUM 200/0** ..... 4¾″
> **200/I** ..... 5½″

Retreat to Safety
In tausend Ängsten
> **HUM 201/2/0** ... 4″
> **201/I** ..... 5½″

Known to have been produced in HUM 201/I size but with decimal point (201.) size indicator (5½″).

Signs of Spring
Frühlingsidyll
> **HUM 203/2/0** .. 4″
> **203/I** ..... 5½″

Known size variations.

HUM 200   Little Goat Herder

HUM 201   Retreat to Safety

HUM 203   Signs of Spring

Weary Wanderer
In Lauterbach hab i . . . ,
    HUM 204 . . . . 6"

**M.I. Hummel Store Plaque
(in German) (CE)**
    HUM 205 . . . . 5½x4"
See variations.

**Holy Water Font, Angel
Cloud**
Weihkessel, Kind mit Blume
    HUM 206 . . . . 2¼x4¾"
Very rare. Bowl designs vary.

Holy Water Font
*Weihkessel, Christkindlein
kommt*
    HUM 207 . . . . 2x4¾"

HUM 204 Weary Wanderer

HUM 205 M.I. Hummel Store Plaque (in German)

HUM 206 Holy Water Font, Angel Cloud

HUM 207 Holy Water Font

**M.I. Hummel Store Plaque
(in French) (CE)**
      HUM 208........5½x4″
See variations.

**M.I. Hummel Store Plaque
(in Swedish) (CE)**
      HUM 209........5½x4″
See variations.

**M.I. Hummel Store Plaque
(in English) (CE)**
      HUM 210........5½x4″

**M.I. Hummel Store Plaque
with Merry Wanderer (CE)**
      HUM 211........5½x4″
See variations.

**M.I. Hummel Store Plaque
(in Spanish) (CE)**
      HUM 213........5½x4″
See variations.

HUM 208 M.I. Hummel Store Plaque (in French)

HUM 209 M.I. Hummel Store Plaque (in Swedish)

HUM 211 M.I. Hummel Store Plaque with Merry Wanderer

HUM 213 M.I. Hummel Store Plaque (in Spanish)

Nativity set with wooden stable
Krippensatz mit Holzstall
  HUM 214

214/A/Maria ......
      6¼″
Virgin Mary
214/A/Kind ....
      1½x3½″
Infant Jesus
214/B ....7½″
Joseph
214/C ....3½″
Angel, standing
214/D ....3″
Angel, kneeling
214/E ....3½″
We Congratulate
214/F .....7″
Shepherd, standing
214/G ....4¾″
Shepherd, kneeling
214/H ....4″
Shepherd, kneeling
with flute
214/J .....5″

Donkey
214/K ....3½x6¼″
Ox
214/L.....8¼″
Moorish King
214/M....5½″
King, kneeling
214/N ....5½″
King, kneeling, with
cashbox
214/O ....1½x2″
Lamb

Has also been produced in white
overglaze and bisque. Is also
produced without wooden
stable.

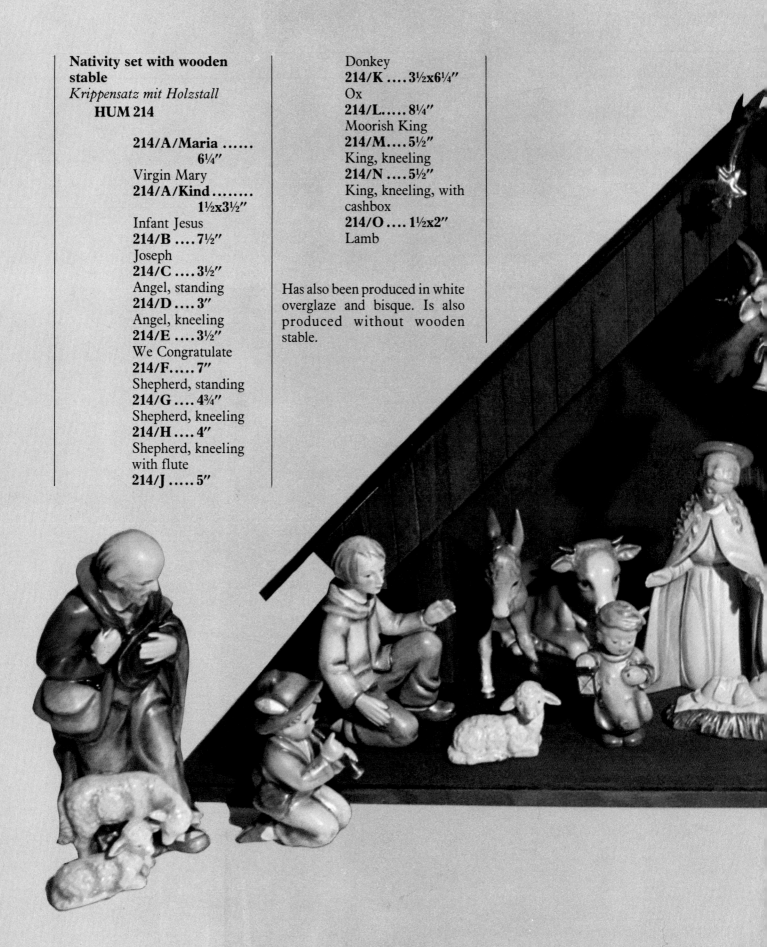

Boy with Toothache
Schmerz lass nach
> **HUM 217.......5½″**

Birthday Serenade
Geburtstagsständchen
> **HUM 218/O ....5¼″**
> **218/2/O . 4¼″**

Old models have boy playing horn, girl playing accordion. Newer models (after 1965) have boy playing accordion, girl playing horn.

We Congratulate
Pärchen
> **HUM 220.......4″**

Same as HUM 214/E but with base.

Madonna Plaque
Maddonenbild
> **HUM 222.......4x5″**

Similar in design to HUM 48.

Table Lamp, To Market
> **HUM 223.......9½″**

HUM 217 Boy with Toothache

HUM 218 Birthday Serenade

HUM 222 Madonna Plaque

HUM 220 We Congratulate

HUM 223 Table Lamp, To Market

**Table Lamp, Wayside
Harmony**
  HUM 224/I ..... 7½″
    224/II .... 9½″

Table Lamp, Just resting
  HUM 225/I ..... 7½″
    225/II .... 9½″

The mail is here
Trara- die Post ist da
  HUM 226........ 4¼x6″

**Table Lamp, She loves me,
she loves me not ...**
  HUM 227........ 7½″

Table Lamp, Good Friends
  HUM 228........ 7½″

HUM 224 Table Lamp, Wayside Harmony HUM 225 Just resting

HUM 226 The mail is here

**HUM 227 Table Lamp,
She loves me, she loves me not . . .**

HUM 228 Table Lamp, Good Friends

153

Table Lamp, Apple Tree Girl
  HUM 229........ 7½″

Table Lamp, Apple Tree Boy
  HUM 230........ 7½″

Table Lamp, Birthday Serenade
  HUM 231........ 9¾″

Table Lamp, Happy Days
  HUM 232........ 9¾″

Table Lamp, Birthday Serenade
  HUM 234........ 7¾″
Same as HUM 231.

Table Lamp, Happy Days
  HUM 235........ 7¾″

Same as HUM 232.

Angel with lute
Engel mit Laute
  HUM 238/A .... 2″

Angel with accordion
Engel mit bandoneon
  HUM 238/B .... 2″

Angel with trumpet
Engel mit trompete
  HUM 238/C .... 2″

HUM 229 Table Lamp, Apple Tree Girl   **HUM 230 Boy**

HUM 235   Table Lamp, Happy Days   **HUM 234   Birthday Serenade**

HUM 238/B/C/A   Angel with accordion   **Angel with trumpet**   **Angel with lute**

Girl with nosegay
Mädchen mit Blumenstrauss
   HUM 239/A .... 3½″

Girl with doll
Mädchen mit Puppe
   HUM 239/B .... 3½″

Boy with horse
Junge mit Holzpferd
   HUM 239/C .... 3½″

Little Drummer
Trommler
   HUM 240........4¼″

Holy Water Font, Madonna and Child
Weihkessel
   HUM 243........3x4″

Holy Water Font, Holy Family
Weihkessel, Heilige Familie
   HUM 246........3¼x4″

Holy Water Font, Guardian Angel
Weihkessel
   HUM 248........2¼x5½″

HUM 239/C/A/B Boy with horse   Girl with nosegay Girl with doll

HUM 240 Little Drummer

HUM 243 Holy Water Font, Madonna and Child

HUM 248 Holy Water Font, Guardian Angel

HUM 246 Holy Water Font, Holy Family

Goatherd, book end
Ziegenbub, Buchstütze
>   HUM 250/A .... 5½"

Feeding Time, book end
Im Hühnerhof, Buchstütze
>   HUM 250/B .... 5½"

She loves me, she loves me not! book end
Liebt mich, liebt mich nicht, Buchstütze
>   HUM 251/B .... 5"

Good Friends, book end
Freunde, Buchstütze
>   HUM 251/A .... 5"

Apple Tree Boy, book end
Herbst, Junge im Baum, Buchstütze
>   HUM 252/B .... 5"

Apple Tree Girl, book end
Frühling, Mädchen im Baum, Buchstütze
>   HUM 252/A .... 5"

A stitch in time
Zwei rechts-zwei links
>   HUM 255........ 6¾"

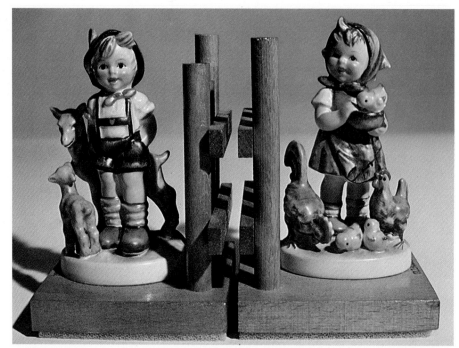

HUM 250/A Goatherd, book end   Feeding Time, book end HUM 250/B

HUM 251/A Good Friends, book end
She loves me, she loves me not! book end HUM 251/B

HUM 252/A Apple Tree Girl, book end   **Apple Tree Boy, book end HUM 252/B**

HUM 255 A stitch in time

Knitting Lesson
Ob's gelingt?
> **HUM 256** . . . . 7½"

For Mother
Fürs Mütterchen
> **HUM 257** . . . . 5"

Which Hand?
Rat mal!
> **HUM 258** . . . . 5½"

HUM 256   Knitting Lesson

HUM 257   For Mother

HUM 258   Which Hand?

Large nativity set with wooden stable

Krippensatz, gross

HUM 260........

260A...... 9¾"
Madonna

260B...... 11¾"
Saint Joseph

260C...... 5¾"
Infant Jesus

260D ..... 5¼"
Good Night

260E...... 4¼"
Angel Serenade

260F...... 6¼"
We Congratulate

260G ..... 11¾"
Shepherd, Standing

260H ..... 3¾"
Sheep standing w/lamb

260J...... 7"
Shepherd Boy, Kneeling

260K...... 5⅛"
Little Tooter

260L...... 7½"
Donkey, Standing

260M ..... 6"x11"
Cow, Lying

260N...... 12¾"
Black King, Standing

260O ..... 12"
King, Standing

260P...... 9"
King, Kneeling

260R...... 3¼"x4"
One Sheep, Lying

Angelic Song
Stille Nacht, ohne Kerzentülle
HUM 261........5″

Heavenly Lullabye
HUM 262........3½x5″

Merry Wanderer, Wall Plaque
HUM 263........4x5¾″ (CE)

HUM 261 Angelic Song

HUM 262 Heavenly Lullabye

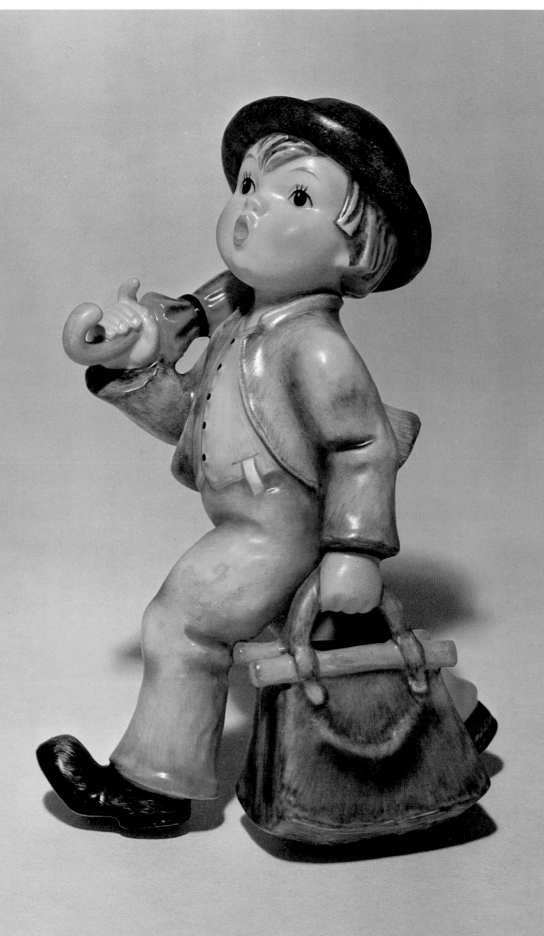

HUM 263 Merry Wanderer, Wall Plaque

**Annual Plate, 1971,
Heavenly Angel**
Jahresteller, 1971
     HUM 264 . . . . 7½″ (CE)

**Annual Plate, 1972, Hear
Ye, Hear Ye**
Jahresteller, 1972
     HUM 265 . . . . 7½″ (CE)

**Annual Plate, 1973,
Globetrotter**
Jahresteller, 1973
     HUM 266 . . . . 7½″ (CE)

**Annual Plate, 1974, Goose
Girl**
Jahresteller, 1974
     HUM 267 . . . . 7½″ (CE)

HUM 264   Annual Plate, 1971, Heavenly Angel

HUM 265   Annual Plate, 1972, Hear Ye, Hear Ye

HUM 266   Annual Plate, 1973, Globetrotter

HUM 267   Annual Plate, 1974, Goose Girl

Annual Plate, 1975, Ride Into Christmas (CE)
Jahresteller, 1975
      HUM 268........7½"

Annual Plate, 1976, Apple Tree Girl
Jahresteller, 1976
      HUM 269........7½"

Annual Plate, 1977, Apple Tree Boy
      HUM 270........7½"

Anniversary Plate, 1975, Stormy Weather
      HUM 280........10" (CE)

HUM 268   Annual Plate, 1975, Ride Into Christmas

HUM 269 Annual Plate, 1976, Apple Tree Girl

HUM 270   Annual Plate, 1977,   Apple Tree Boy

HUM 280   Anniversary Plate, 1975, Stormy Weather

The Artist
Kunstmaler
HUM 304........5½″

The Builder
Der Schwerarbeiter
HUM 305........5½″

Little Bookkeeper
Stellvertretung
HUM 306........4¾″

Good Hunting!
Weidmannsheil!
HUM 307........5″

Little Tailor
Schneiderlein
HUM 308........5½″
Known size variations.

HUM 304   The Artist

HUM 305   The Builder

HUM 306   Little Bookkeeper

HUM 307   Good Hunting!

HUM 308   Little Tailor

Kiss Me!
Hab' mich lieb!
    HUM 311........6″

Confidentially
Zweigespräch
    HUM 314........5½″
No bow tie on older models.
Newer models have red bow tie.

Mountaineer
I' hab's erreicht
    HUM 315........5″

Not for you!
Nix für dich!
    HUM 317........6″

Doll Bath
Puppenbad
    HUM 319........5″

HUM 311   Kiss Me!

HUM 314 Confidentially

HUM 317 Not for you!

HUM 315 Mountaineer

HUM 319 Doll Bath

173

Wash Day
Grosse Wäsche
     HUM 321........6″
Known size variations.

Little Pharmacist
Der Apotheker
     HUM 322........6″
Known variations on bottle label.

The Run-a-way
Der frohe Wanderer
     HUM 327........5¼″
Known size variations.

Carnival
Fastnach
     HUM 328........5¾″

HUM 321 Wash Day

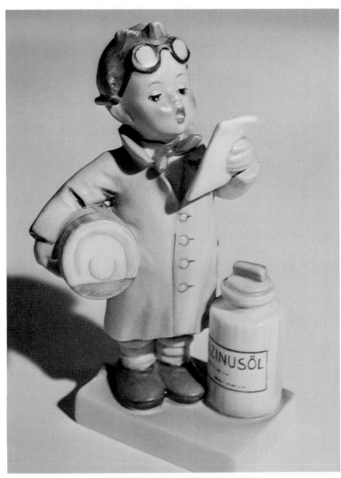

HUM 322   Little Pharmacist

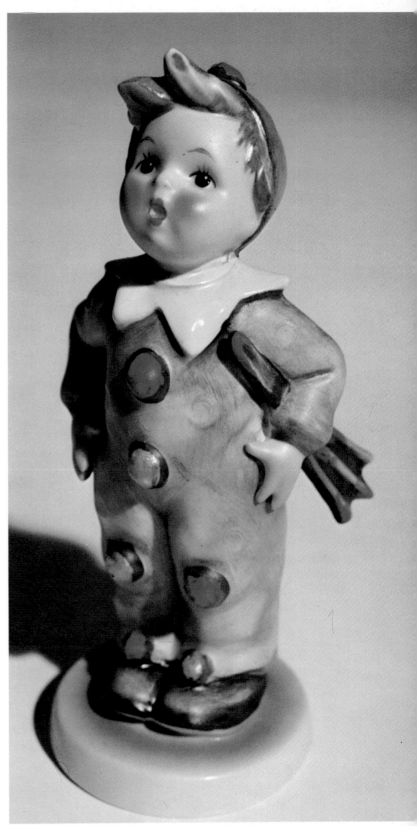

HUM 328   Carnival

HUM 327   The Run-a-way

Crossroads
Am Scheideweg
     HUM 331........ 6¾″

Soldier Boy
Stillgestanden!
     HUM 332........ 6″

HUM 331 Crossroads

HUM 332   Soldier Boy

Blessed event
Das grosse Ereignis
    HUM 333........5½″

Homeward Bound
Heimkehr vom Felde
    HUM 334........5¼″
Older models have support post
under goat.

Close Harmony
Geburtstagsständchen
    HUM 336........5½″

Cinderella
Aschenputtel
    HUM 337........4½″

HUM 333 Blessed event

HUM 334 Homeward Bound

HUM 336 Close Harmony

HUM 337 Cinderella

Letter to Santa Claus
Brief an Christkind
   HUM 340........7¼″

Mischief Maker
Der Störenfried
   HUM 342........5″

Feathered Friends
Schwanenteich
   HUM 344........4¾″

A Fair Measure
Der Kaufmann
   HUM 345........5½″

HUM 340 Letter to Santa Claus

HUM 342 Mischief Maker

HUM 345 A Fair Measure

HUM 344 Feathered Friends

The smart Little Sister
Das kluge Schwesterlein
        HUM 346........ 4¾″

Adventure Bound, The Seven Swabians
Die Sieben Schwaben
        HUM 347........ 7½x8¼″

HUM 346   The smart Little Sister

HUM 347 Adventure Bound, The Seven Swabians

Ring Around the Rosie
Ringelreihen
      HUM 348........ 6¾″

Spring Dance
Sommertanz
      HUM 353/O .... 5¼″
          353/I ..... 6¾″
Smaller size considered rare.

Autumn Harvest
Herbstegen
      HUM 355........ 4¾″

HUM 348   Ring Around the Rosie

HUM 353 Spring Dance

HUM 355 Autumn Harvest

Gay Adventure
Frohes Wandern
     HUM 356........5″
Was called Joyful Adventure in
older catalogs.

Guiding Angel
Kniender Engel mit Lanterne
     HUM 357........2¾″

Shining Light
Kniender Engel mit Kerze
     HUM 358........2¾″

Tuneful Angel
Kniender Engel mit Horn
     HUM 359........2¾″

HUM 356 Gay Adventure

HUM 357 Guiding Angel   **HUM 358 Shining Light**   **HUM 359   Tuneful Angel**

Wall Vase, Boy and Girl
Wandvase, Junge und Mädchen
     HUM 360 A..... 4½x6¼″
Considered rare.

Wall Vase, Boy
     HUM 360 B..... 4½x6¼″
Considered rare.

Wall Vase, Girl
     HUM 360 C..... 4½x6¼″
Considered rare

HUM 360 A   Wall Vase, Boy and Girl

HUM 360 B   Wall Vase, Boy

HUM 360 C   Wall Vase, Girl

Favorite Pet
Ostergruss
    HUM 361........4½″

Big Housecleaning
Grossreinmachen
    HUM 363........4″

Flying Angel
Hängeengel
    HUM 366

Same angel that flies above HUM 214 nativity set. See photo of HUM 214. Known to have been produced in white overglaze.

Busy Student
Musterschülerin
    HUM 367........4¼″

Follow the Leader
Mach mit
    HUM 369........7″

Lost Stocking
Hab mein Strumpf verloren
    HUM 374........4¼″

HUM 361 Favorite Pet

HUM 363 Big Housecleaning

HUM 367 Busy Student

HUM 369 Follow the Leader

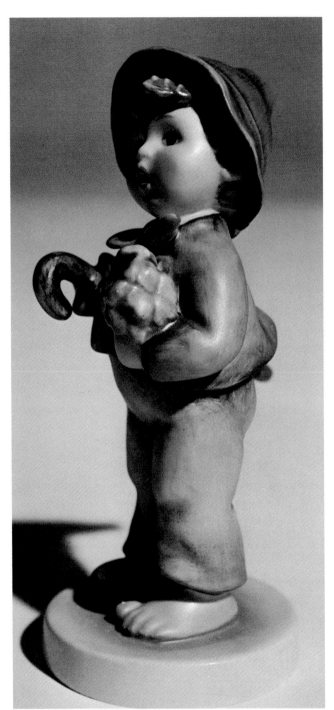

HUM 374 Lost Stocking

Bashful!
Vergissmeinnicht
      HUM 377 . . . . 4¾″

Easter Greetings!
Ostergruss
      HUM 378 . . . . 5¼″

HUM 377 Bashful!

HUM 378 Easter Greetings!

Flower Vendor
Zum Blumenmarkt
HUM 381........5¼″

Visiting an Invalid
Krankenbesuch
HUM 382........5″

Easter Time
Osterfreunde
HUM 384........4″

Chicken-Licken!
Kükenliesl
HUM 385........4¾″

HUM 381 Flower Vendor

HUM 382 Visiting an Invalid

HUM 385 Chicken-Licken!

HUM 384 Easter Time

On Secret Path
Auf heimlichen wegen
        HUM 386........5¼″

**Candlestick on Music Box,
Little Band**
*Leuchter-Kindergruppe auf
Musikdose*
        HUM 388/M....3x4¾″

Candlestick, Little Band
Leuchter Kindergruppe
        HUM 388........3x4¾″
Same as HUM 388/M but
without music box.

Girl with sheet of music
Mädchen mit Notenblatt
        HUM 389........2¼″

Boy with accordion
Junge mit Bandoneon
        HUM 390........2¼″

Girl with trumpet
Mädchen mit Trompete
        HUM 391........2¼″

HUM 386 On Secret Path

HUM 388/M Candlestick on Music Box, Little Band

HUM 391 Girl with trumpet   **HUM 390 Boy with accordion**   **HUM 389 Girl with sheet of music**

Group of Children
Kindergruppe
>   HUM 392........3x4¾″

Group of children on music box.
Kindergruppe mit Musikwerk.
>   HUM 392/M....3x4¾″

Same as HUM 392 but sitting atop music box.

Ride into Christmas
Fahrt in die Weihnacht
>   HUM 396........5¾″

HUM 392 Group of Children

HUM 396 Ride into Christmas

CHAPTER 7: VARIATIONS, MINT ERRORS & FAKES

Every collector should "know his Hummel figurines." Included in this chapter are all variations of "M.I. Hummel" figurines known to exist, including rare "mint errors" sought after by advanced collectors. Also included are photographs of pieces which closely resemble "M.I. Hummel" figurines but, in fact, should not be confused with genuine "M.I. Hummel" figurines at all.

Old and new variations of HUM 154 The Waiter. Note that the newer model (right) carries a bottle of "Rhein wine" on its tray, and the older model (left) carries a bottle of wine whose label is difficult to read.

Variations in the suspenders of HUM 6 Sensitive Hunter. Note that older model (left) has parallel-strap suspenders and that the newer model (right) has crossed-strap suspenders.

Collectors of "M.I. Hummel" figurines frequently want to know why there are variations involving sizes, colors, names, designations, and the actual appearances of differing models with the same number.

The overall answer should not be surprising: Just as with stamps, coins, and limited editions, there are changes and errors during production which are often highly appealing to serious collectors. For example, "inverted" stamps and "mint error" coins are legendary among collectors and auctioneers. In fact, it is often a collector's dream to one day discover an example which is different from the norm.

"M.I. Hummel" figurines are no exception. Prolific collectors scour the world looking for unusual and obvious variations. Some are errors, some are not. That is why this chapter has been assembled, as a *general guide* to *known* variations and "mint errors" involving "M.I. Hummel" figurines.

Still, the reader must remember that additional variations and errors are bound to be found in future "M.I. Hummel" collecting, just as the U.S. Mint will still turn out the occasional oddity. These discoveries add a new dimension to every collector's fund of information.

Here, now, are general guidelines.

COLOR VARIATION

Variations in the colors of "M.I. Hummel" figurines have occurred for a variety of reasons, which fall into three basic categories: unrecorded variations, authorized production changes, and simple aging.

Unrecorded variations have been noted by many collectors, especially in the area of madonnas and other religious figurines. The majority of these variations are in white overglaze, white bisque, and the fully painted figurines. The highly detailed hand painting process finds no two artists with exactly the same style. As a result, minor unrecorded variations may occur. Though white overglaze and white bisque variations appear throughout the entire "M.I. Hummel" collection, they are considered to be very rare. Unrecorded variations are those not authorized for production by W. Goebel.

Production and model changes have been continually taking place since "M.I. Hummel" figurines first appeared on the market in 1935. These changes can concern themselves with color, design, or size. They can also come about through development of new ceramic paints by the W. Goebel chemical laboratory.

For example, in efforts to brighten the appearance of the figurine faces, W. Goebel developed a brighter red paint for the lips of the figurines. Individual cases of color change always have tended to brighten the appearance of a particular figurine, and in general, the development of new metallic oxide paints since the mid-1950s has set figurines of more recent manufacture apart from their older counterparts.

Aging of old figurines occurs due to the chemical composition of their ceramic mass, and due to the atmospheric conditions of the area where the figurines are kept. The basic molecular compositon of the various clays, kaolins, feldspars, and quartzes employed in the milling of the ceramic mass change from pit to pit, mine to mine, and region to region. As a result, colors tend to dull or mellow on figurines manufactured prior to the mid-1950s. Developments by W. Goebel chemists since this period have enabled the factory to produce "M.I. Hummel" figurines and other collectors items in bright, exciting colors which offer lasting beauty that will not fade, dull, or mellow for either chemical or atmospheric reasons.

NAME VARIATION

The names originally applied to some "M.I. Hummel" figurines in early catalogs have been changed. The reason for this was a switch from pure translation to transliteration, that is translating according to the idea or theme rather than the literal meaning of the original German. For example, figurine HUM 142 Apple Tree Boy was originally called Fall in English. Since name changes do not directly affect the figurines themselves, they are considered of minor importance to serious collectors.

MODEL VARIATION

Model variations, both authorized and unknown, are of special interest to serious collectors. The reason for this is that they offer the collector the opportunity to possess unique figurines. These rarities are, in most cases, the result of production changes during the early years of their appearance or unknown errors during the production process. Because of the widespread interest in these unique figurines, a substantial portion of this chapter is devoted to a full-color visual record of those pieces known to exist.

BASE VARIATION

Occasionally, collectors will come across two figurines identical except for the bases. From time to time, the W. Goebel firm has changed the design of its "M.I. Hummel" figurine bases for better support and visual compatibility with the figurines themselves. Also, a figurine base will often change if a particular model is redesigned. Contrary to rumor, the W. Goebel firm has never maintained stockpiles of standard "M.I. Hummel" figurine bases. Each figurine has a specially designed base to complement its style.

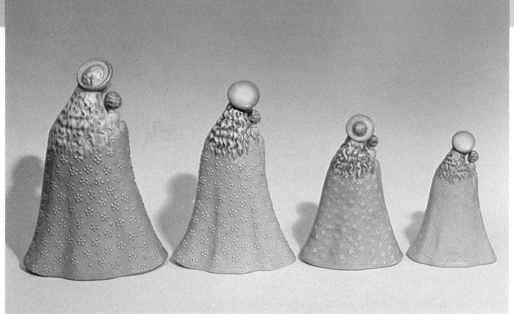

HUM 10 Flower Madonna with child. Notice design variations of cap and halo on rear view.

Old and new production models of HUM 22 Sitting Angel holy water font. The base of this font was redesigned, eliminating the ridge along the bottom of the water bowl. The larger of the two newer models (far right) also has noticeable color variations.

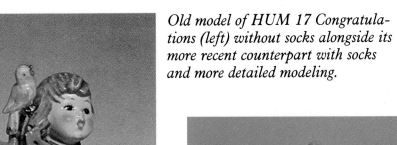

Old model of HUM 17 Congratulations (left) without socks alongside its more recent counterpart with socks and more detailed modeling.

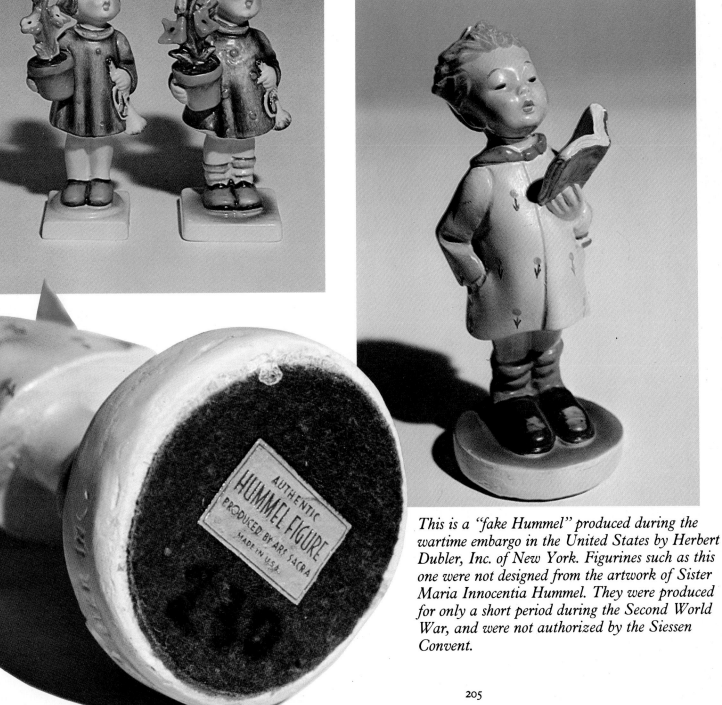

This is a "fake Hummel" produced during the wartime embargo in the United States by Herbert Dubler, Inc. of New York. Figurines such as this one were not designed from the artwork of Sister Maria Innocentia Hummel. They were produced for only a short period during the Second World War, and were not authorized by the Siessen Convent.

205

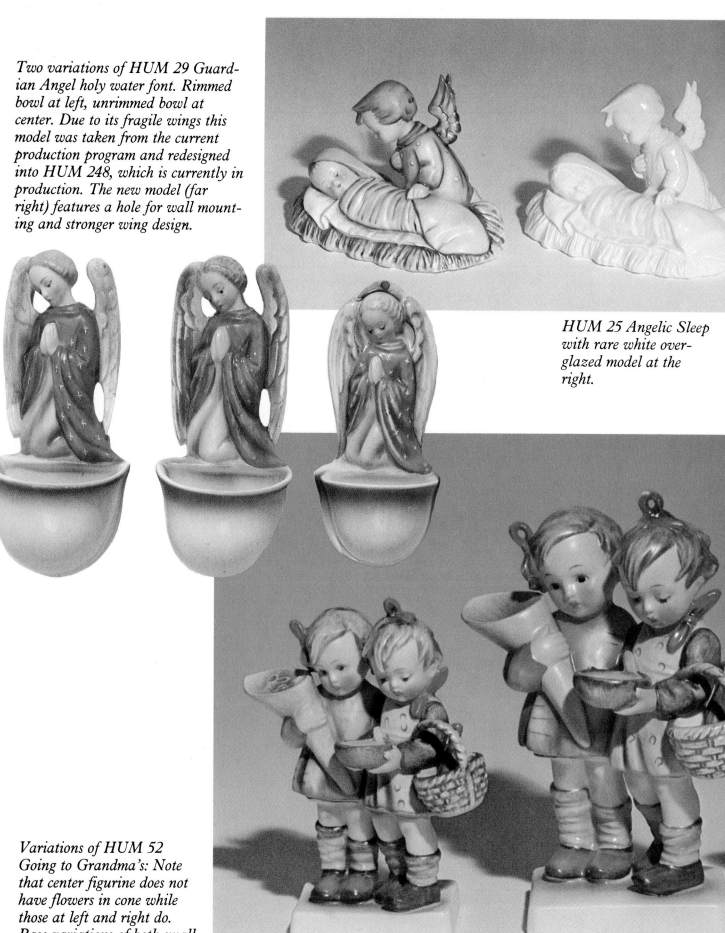

Two variations of HUM 29 Guardian Angel holy water font. Rimmed bowl at left, unrimmed bowl at center. Due to its fragile wings this model was taken from the current production program and redesigned into HUM 248, which is currently in production. The new model (far right) features a hole for wall mounting and stronger wing design.

HUM 25 Angelic Sleep with rare white overglazed model at the right.

Variations of HUM 52 Going to Grandma's: Note that center figurine does not have flowers in cone while those at left and right do. Base variations of both small models, rectangular at left, oval at right.

HUM 71, the famous Stormy Weather
at left. On the right is a Japanese fake.
Original at left bears the lead factory
archive seal.

HUM 72 Spring Cheer in old (left) and new (right) color and
design variations. Older model does not hold flower in right hand
while newer model does.

Lid and bowl design variations on old (left) and new (right) models of HUM III/57 Chick Girl box.

HUM 57 Chick Girl with design variation. Note that smaller model (right) contains less chicks in its basket than its larger counterpart.

Three color variations of HUM 78 Infant of Krumbad. Left to right: flesh bisque, colorized, and white overglaze.

Design variations of HUM 79 Globe Trotter: Newer model (left in both photographs) has a different type of basket weave on boy's basket.

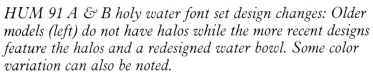

HUM 91 A & B holy water font set design changes: Older models (left) do not have halos while the more recent designs feature the halos and a redesigned water bowl. Some color variation can also be noted.

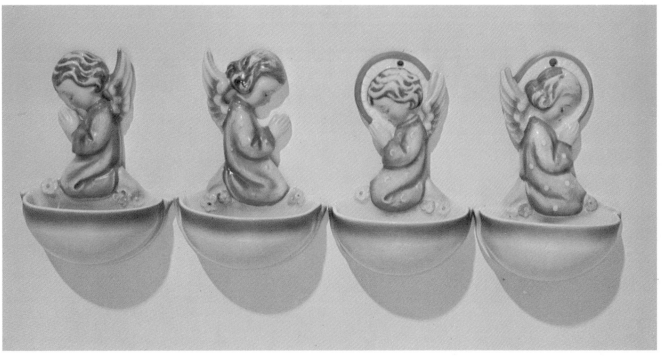

Old (left) and new (right) design variations of HUM 172 & 173 Festival Harmony. On old models there are flowers growing up to the knees of both angels. On the new models the flowers do not climb higher than the bottom of the vestments. On old model of HUM 172 (left side, second figurine) the bird is in the flowers. On the new model (right side, second figurine) it is not. New model HUM 173 plays flute while old model flute player was 172. New model HUM 172 now plays mandolin but previously played flute as HUM 173.

HUM 1 Puppy Love (left) accompanied by Japanese fake (right).

Two variations in the newspaper of HUM 184 Latest News. Bermuda News (right) was one of the many newspaper names used in the manufacture of this popular figurine. Today, all production models bear the name Das Allerneuste.

Old (left) and new (right) "M.I. Hummel" store plaques. These have appeared in several designs and languages. See chapter six for the full collection under appropriate HUM numbers.

HUM 114 ashtray Let's
Sing design variation:
old (left) with boy on
right side, new (right)
with boy on left side.

Rare blue cloaked (left) and white overglaze
(right) color variations of the HUM 151
madonna.

Color and design variations
of the famous HUM 124
Chef, Hello. Old model
(left) has darker trousers
and is smaller. Newer model
(right) has brighter trousers
and is larger.

*The famed HUM 153 Auf Wiedersehen in two size variations
(left and center) alongside an extremely rare version of the
figurine (far right) in which the waving boy is wearing a
Tyrolean cap.*

*Design variations of HUM
218 Birthday Serenade. In
older models (center and
far right) the boy plays the
flute and the girl plays the
accordion. In the new
model (left) the girl plays
the flute and the boy plays
the accordion.*

Variations in the name on the medicine bottles of HUM 322 Little Pharmacist. At the left, in German, bottle reads "Rizinusöl." At right, in English, it reads "Vitamins."

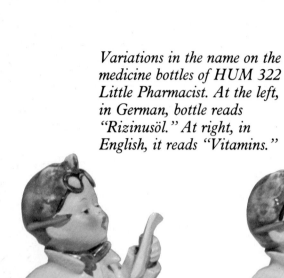

Design variations on HUM 314 Confidentially. Older model (left) has a cactus on a smaller pedestal than the newer model (right). Newer model appears with boy wearing bow tie.

Design variations on HUM 334 Homeward Bound. Older model (left) appeared with a support pedestal under the goat. New model (right) is manufactured without the support post.

HUM 59 Skier (left) with Japanese fake (right).

Color and design changes in HUM 327 The Run-a-way. Old model (left) has objects protruding from rucksack and a different positioning of the shoes. New model (right) has a different colored shirt than his older counterpart.

HUM 353/I Spring Dance at left. At the right is HUM 353/O, its rare, smaller-size variation.

CHAPTER
8: HISTORY & EXPLANATION OF MARKS & SYMBOLS

The first Goebel trademark was designed in 1871 by Franz-Detleff Goebel and was stamped onto his Thuringer Ware. It changed several times prior to the appearance of "M.I. Hummel" figurines in 1935, and has been redesigned many times since. For the collector, trademarks are the only means of identifying the era of production of the figurines.

The following is a concise documentation of all Goebel trademarks authorized for use on "M.I. Hummel" figurines, and, subsequently, other collectors products. In his search for accurate documentation of all Goebel trademarks used in conjunction with "M.I. Hummel" figurines, the author made a thorough investigation of W. Goebel's archive and queried the world's leading collectors on the subject. But, as is the case with other aspects of "M.I. Hummel" figurine collecting, it is always possible that a few rare and undocumented variations may exist.

1935

The year 1935 marked the debut of "M.I. Hummel" figurines. The trademark in use at the time was the "1923 Wide Crown WG." This trademark was the first ever used on an "M.I. Hummel" figurine, appearing in the following variations on the bottom of the figurine bases:

     1.) Incised without color.
     2.) Underglazed in blue or black.
     3.) Underglazed and incised.

FIGURINES BEARING ANY OF THESE VARIATIONS WERE MANUFACTURED BETWEEN 1935 AND 1937.

1937

Franz Goebel designed a new crown trademark featuring a narrower crown with "Goebel" in script. This "narrow crown" trademark replaced the 1923 Wide Crown WG, but on many figurines both the wide crown and narrow crown appeared. This is known as the "double crown" variation. The trademarks continued to be affixed to the bottom of the figurine bases in the following manner:

     1.) Incised without color.
     2.) Underglazed in blue or black.
     3.) Underglazed and incised.

During the war years, a limited number of figurines were produced. Contrary to rumors, there was no production of "M.I. Hummel" figurines redesigned to incorporate Nazi themes. The principle effort of the factory during the war years involved the production of basic tableware and a very limited quantity of nonpolitical collector objects for the home market.

THE "NARROW CROWN" TRADEMARK AND THE "DOUBLE CROWN" VARIATION DESIGNATE FIGURINES PRODUCED FROM 1937 THROUGH 1945.

1946

With the approval of the U.S. Military Government in Germany, W. Goebel was allowed to export "M.I. Hummel" figurines with the stipulation that "U.S.-Zone Germany" or "U.S. Zone" appeared on the bottom of the figurine bases

U.S.-Zone Germany

U.S.-Zone Germany

with the trademark. There was no change from the 1937 trademark pattern, and most of the 1937 crown variations can be found with the U.S. Zone markings. Generally, the U.S. Zone was underglazed, but it also appeared rubber stamped over the glaze. Some collectors have attempted to remove the U.S. Zone markings from the figurines with the hope of passing them off to less-knowledgeable collectors as prewar pieces. This can always be checked by holding the figurine to a light source and tilting it a bit, looking for a fault or abrasion in the glazing that will always be present if the U.S. Zone has been eradicated. According to W. Goebel officials, the formula of their glaze has been and continues to be a well-kept secret which nobody has been able to duplicate when covering over an eradicated or altered trademark. The 1946 era trademarks are often difficult to distinguish because they were poorly incised into the figurine bases. Few 1946 era trademarks were underglazed because of the difficulty in obtaining decals after the war.

THE "U.S. ZONE" VARIATIONS WERE PRODUCED FROM 1946 THROUGH 1948.

1949

The year 1949 saw the birth of the Federal Republic of Germany, modern-day West Germany. The U.S. Zone markings were replaced by "West Germany" block printed in black underglaze. Sometimes it was stamped over the glaze, making it possible to scrape off or eradicate the West Germany and fraudulently pass the figurines off as prewar. Collectors should check carefully and be wary of prewar figurines with irregularities in the glazing on the bottom of the figurine bases. The 1937 trademark and its crown variations were used with West Germany in 1949 only. In addition to the 1949 trademark, a small "WG" was incised on the side or the top of the base of some models, appearing to the right of the "M.I. Hummel" signature.

1950

In 1950 Franz Goebel designed the bee trademark. This large "full bee" often appeared alongside and in conjunction with the 1937 crown variations. The full bee appeared on the bottom of the figurine bases in black or blue and sometimes green or magenta underglaze, flying in the crutch of a "V" device. On some models, the full bee was both underglazed and incised.
"FULL BEE" TRADEMARKS AND THEIR VARIATIONS APPEARED DURING THE YEARS 1950 THROUGH 1955.

1956

In 1956 the Goebel trademark was changed to the "small bee." Franz Goebel designed this small bee to be smaller than the full bee, though still inside the "V" device. It was underglazed in both black and blue. The small bee appeared only in 1956 and marked the end of the appearance of the 1937 crown variations on postwar figurines.

1957

1957 saw the appearance of the "high bee," so called because the bee itself flew higher inside the "V" device than its 1950 and 1956 predecessors. It was also in-between the 1950 and 1956 bees in size. The high bee was underglazed in both black and blue, and designated figurines manufactured in 1957.

1958

A much smaller bee was introduced as the trademark for 1958, fitting deeply into the crutch of the "V" device. Appearing in black or blue underglaze, this "baby bee" identified all figurines manufactured during 1958.

1959

In 1959 Franz Goebel designed a new bee trademark, the "vee bee," so called because of the more definite "V" shape of its bee wings. Similar in size to the 1958 baby bee, the vee bee has more sharply angular wings, but remains centered in the crutch of the "V" trademark device. Underglazed in both black and blue, the vee bee identifies figurines manufactured in 1959.

1960

Once again the Goebel trademark was redesigned by Franz Goebel. This new design, the "new bee," featured a stylized bee and a much thicker "V" device. In many cases, the "R" registered trademark annotation can be found alongside it. Appearing in black or blue underglaze, the new bee designated figurines manufactured from 1960 until 1972.

1972

In 1972 a new Goebel trademark was created, combining the Goebel name with the previous trademark. This new "Goebel bee" is the trademark currently in use by the W. Goebel firm in the manufacture of "M.I. Hummel" figurines and other collectors items. It usually appears in blue underglaze on the bottom of the figurine base. The new Goebel bee trademark denotes figurines manufactured during the present era, beginning in 1972.

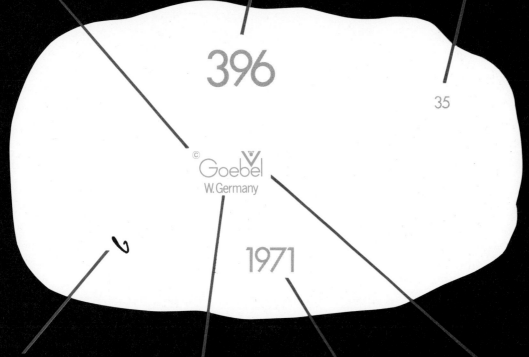

The copyright © to the left of the W. Goebel trademark indicates that this particular figurine is protected by U.S. copyright laws.

This is the figurine identification number. It is the official means of identifying all figurines produced by W. Goebel. Here, for example, we find HUM 396, otherwise known as Ride into Christmas. Since it has only been manufactured in one size (5¾") it does not carry a size designator. Size designators appear to the right of the figurine identification number, set off by a slash.

This incised number cannot help you to identify or date your figurine. It is simply a control number used by W. Goebel's molding department during periodic quality checks.

This painted and overglazed symbol cannot help you to identify or date your figurine. It is the symbol used by one of W. Goebel's master painters to approve the artistry of the figurine during one of the many quality control checks.

The "W. Germany," though sitting directly below the W. Goebel trademark, is not part of the trademark design. It is present to legally establish the country of origin of the "M.I. Hummel" figurines for export purposes.

This is the current W. Goebel trademark. It is used on "M.I. Hummel" figurines and other collectors objects.

This date, below the W. Goebel trademark, indicates the year of copyright publication of the particular figurine model.

SIZE DESIGNATORS

Since the beginning of production, "M.I. Hummel" figurines have been manufactured in numerous official sizes. Some models have been made in more sizes than others, but there is no single reason for this.

As a result of the varying sizes, a marking system has evolved over the years to designate variations within a particular model. In addition to officially authorized variations in size, there are many examples of "mold growth" figurines made during the pre-1954 era when plaster of paris was used for working models. Since 1954, the use of acrylic resin for modeling has led to greater uniformity in the figurines themselves.

When each model is first made, the first size decided upon for production becomes the "standard" of that model. On early figurines, this was designated on the bottom by a "0" appearing after a slash following the model number. For example, HUM 47 (Goose Girl—first made in the 1930s) in the standard size (4¾") has the marking 47/0. But not all standard sizes of all figurines use the "0."

The designation "0" appeared with the first figurines in 1935 and was used for the last time with HUM 218 Birthday Serenade, after which it was dropped as a designation of the standard size for all subsequent model numbers. (Note: there has been one exception—HUM 352 Spring Dance, which has been manufactured in a 352/0 size. As a result, this figurine has earned a reputation among collectors as a rare model.) No substitution for the "0" was made. Thus, no figurines numbered higher than HUM 218 carry any designation for the standard size of each.

Prior to its elimination from the size designation system, the "0" appeared to the right of the Arabic number markings used to designate models smaller than the standard size. In the case of larger variations of the same model, the "0" never followed the Roman numerals. The subsequent designator is now usually either a Roman numeral or an Arabic number.

Figurines larger than the "0" size are designated by Roman numerals in ascending order from I to X. Size I is therefore larger than size "0" with the general rule being that the larger the Roman numeral, the greater the size of the figurine. This does not guarantee that two figurines of the same model number with the same size designation—II for example—will be of the same height due to the slight growth of the old plaster working models used prior to 1954. It is also possible that a figurine model has been redesigned, re-master molded, reapproved by the Siessen Convent, and come out of production different in size than its older counterpart of the same size designation. In the past two decades, the W. Goebel firm has made great strides in the area of standardization of its "M.I. Hummel" figurines, but due to the growth of the old plaster of paris working models and the enormous redesigning effort that took place when the firm began gearing up for production after the end of the Second World War, it is possible that a collector will run into minor size variations within the same model that have the same size designation.

Figurines smaller than the "0" size are designated by Arabic numbers in ascending order from 1 upward. This designation generally appears on the bottom of the base and to the right of the model number, set off by a slash. In some special cases, however, the Arabic number will precede the model number. The rule is the larger the Arabic number, the smaller the figurine size. After the Arabic size designation there is another slash, followed by a zero. The presence of this zero to the right of the designation indicates that the figurine in question is smaller than the "0" size. Roman numeral indicators *are not* followed by a zero.

Here are a couple of examples:

195/2/0–"M.I. Hummel" figurine 195, "Barnyard Hero"
size 4 inches

195/I–"M.I. Hummel" figurine 195, "Barnyard Hero"
size 5½ inches

Note that HUM 195/2/0 is smaller than its counterpart, HUM 195/I, which has a Roman numeral size designation.

The size designation system can be best demonstrated by this key:

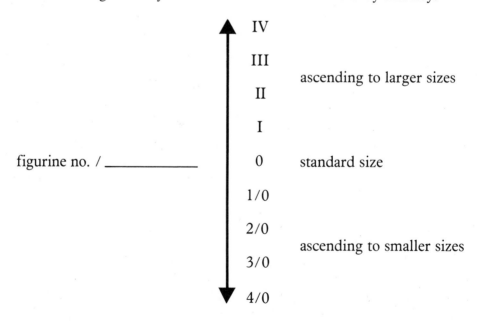

In understanding the size designation system of "M.I. Hummel" figurines, it is important to remember that the designations apply differently to each specific figurine model, but that generally larger and smaller sizes of the same model are specified by the designation key.

VARIATIONS: Candleholders and Boxes

"M.I. Hummel" candy boxes, music boxes, and candleholders differ from the figurines because the size of the candleholder or the size of the box appears *before* the figurine model number, or to the left of it.

Example: HUM 110/0 is the figurine "Let's Sing," but HUM III/110 is the box "Let's Sing" based upon the design of HUM 110.

SPECIAL CASES: Numbers and Markings Which May Confuse

a.) HUM 78, "The Infant of Krumbad," has been produced both in white overglaze and in color. It has been given color designation numbers, which appear *after* the size designation and are preceded by a slash as follows:

HUM 78/ size / paint

The paint numbers will either be 11 for color or 83 for white overglaze.

b.) Markings that appear on the base bottoms of some "M.I. Hummel" figurines in underglaze in the form of initials or small numbers and may confuse collectors, indicate the numerical or signature code of a particular molding department supervisor or master painter who supervised that phase of the figurine manufacture. These markings in no way refer to the year of production, model number, or size designation.

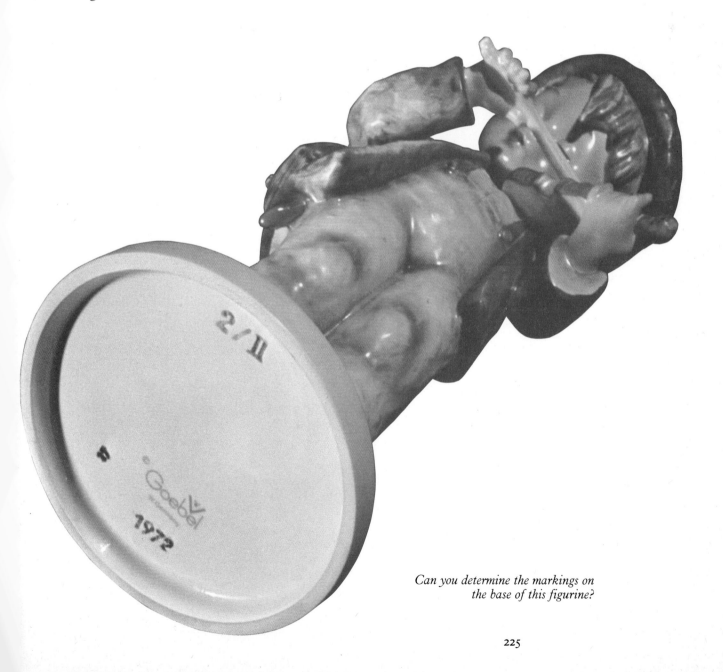

*Can you determine the markings on
the base of this figurine?*

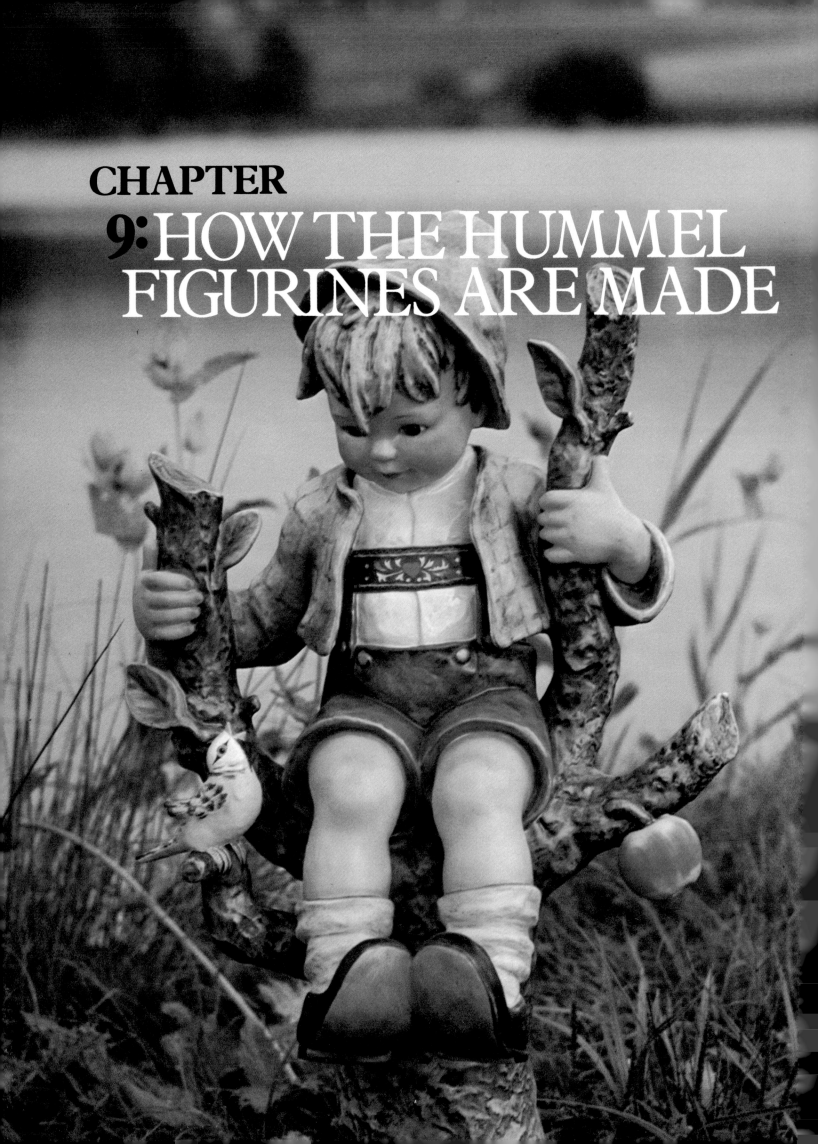

CHAPTER
9: HOW THE HUMMEL FIGURINES ARE MADE

Good collectors should have a thorough knowledge of their collectibles, valuing the work that went into making them just as they value the objects themselves. In a world where handcraftsmanship is rapidly disappearing, the W. Goebel firm, sole manufacturers of "M.I. Hummel" figurines and plates under exclusive license from the Siessen Convent, has continued to follow the two-century-old tradition of porcelain and ceramic manufacture that was developed in its Thuringian homeland shortly before the American Revolution. A work force of 1,500 operates as a team at the Goebel factory in the town of Rödental to produce "M.I. Hummel" figurines, plates, and other collector items. The manufacturing process of an "M.I. Hummel" figurine involves over 700 painstaking hand operations and twenty-five quality control checks. To better understand what goes into the making of an "M.I. Hummel" figurine, it is essential to describe its manufacture step-by-step.

MODELING

The basis for the creation of an "M.I. Hummel" figurine is the collection of drawings and sketches by Sister Maria Innocentia Hummel provided to the W. Goebel firm under special agreement with the Siessen Convent. W. Goebel's chief designer then studies Sister Innocentia's artwork and begins the time-consuming process of creating a clay model that rigidly conforms in color and form to Sister Innocentia's design. Once the original clay model is completed, it is presented to the Siessen Convent for approval. Sometimes the Convent will ask the designer to make minor changes, other times not. After the model has been approved by the Convent, the design must be officially authorized by the directors of the W. Goebel firm for release into the current production program.

At the time of her death in 1946, Sister Innocentia left a large collectin of drawings and sketches belonging to the Siessen Convent, but only some of these have been made into figurines. A flurry of these designs appeared shortly after the end of World War II. At that time, the U.S. Military Government of Germany, having jurisdiction over the Coburg area, the town of Oeslau, and the Goebel firm, granted W. Goebel permission to manufacture and export "M.I. Hummel" figurines and other collectors' items, which lifted the prewar embargo of 1939.

The town of Oeslau, which today has been annexed into the incorporated community of Rödental, was part of the *Kreis* (county) Coburg and the German state of Thuringia until 1920, when the *Kreis* Coburg was ceded to the free state of Bavaria.

After the great postwar boom of new figurine designs, the next new figurines, six designs, made their debut at the New York World's Fair during 1964 and 1965. The most recent appearance of new "M.I. Hummel" figurines took place at the one-hundredth anniversary of the W. Goebel firm in Rödental, West Germany, in 1971 when seven new models were put into production and the first W. Goebel Annual Plate was introduced.

It is important to remember that the approval of a design model by the Siessen Convent does not mean that the particular figurine model will be immediately put into the W. Goebel current production program. When and how many new "M.I. Hummel" figurines are released is a closely guarded company secret.

2 MOLDMAKING

Once the new design is approved for production, the chief designer cuts the original clay model into parts. This is done to facilitate their easy removal from the first molding in plaster of paris—the mother mold, or *Mutterform* in the language of the German porcelain and ceramic trade—and to give the figurines a flow and animation that would be impossible to achieve if they were molded as one piece.

From the mother mold, mother models *(Muttermodellen)*, also of plaster of paris, are created. Craftsmen then carve fine details into these mother models in correspondence with the original clay model. From the mother models, plaster of paris forms *(Modellformen)* are made.

Then, a special acrylic resin *(Kunstharz)* is poured around the plaster of paris model form to create the acrylic working model *(Arbeitsmodell)*. Prior to 1954, these working models were made only of plaster of paris and tended to "grow" slightly. But W. Goebel research, pioneering the acrylic resin process, established a new standard of exactness for achieving uniform figurine size. From these acrylic resin working models, the plaster of paris working molds are formed *(Arbeitsformen)*.

Finally, from the working molds the actual pieces are created.

3 POURING

Liquid ceramic material, referred to in the trade as "slip" is pumped through factory pipelines from the batching room to the molding department, where workers force the slip into the working molds with special injection guns. This slip is a special blend of materials formulated by the W. Goebel ceramic chemists at the factory laboratory to meet the hardness and durability standards required in the manufacture of "M.I. Hummel" figurines.

The composition of this ceramic material includes kaolin from England, feldspar from Norway, clay from the Westerwald region of West Germany, and quartz from both West Germany and Norway. These elements are blended together and milled for about eight hours in huge cylindrical mixers filled with special French and Belgian millstones. After the mixing process, the ceramic material is quality checked and sent through a demagnitizer to make sure that no iron specks find their way into the figurines. Upon reaching the molding department, the material is injected into forms.

Absorbing water from the liquid ceramic material, the working mold leaves a solid ceramic shell on its inner walls. After about twenty minutes, the shell hardens sufficiently, obtains crisp detail, and is removed from the mold by hand. Each mold can be utilized for twenty to twenty-five pourings before water absorbtion causes so much expansion that it

must be discarded to avoid discrepancies in the accuracy of detail. A fresh plaster of paris mold is then put on the production line. This constant changing of the plaster of paris molds helps to control the uniformity of "M.I. Hummel" figurines.

Prior to 1954 the W. Goebel firm and the porcelain and ceramic industries in general were all making their working models out of plaster of paris. These working models lost their detail very quickly and though they were frequently replaced, the walls of the plaster of paris model expanded about 1 per cent each pouring. As a result, prior to 1954 "M.I. Hummel" figurines sometimes "grew" anywhere between ten and twenty per cent. This accounts for height variations which many collectors have noted on some of their older figurines when comparing them with newer figurines of the same model. The introduction of acrylic resin working models pioneered by W. Goebel research in 1954 eliminated this problem, giving the figurines much more detail while retaining a standard size. This development soon spread through the entire industry.

4 GARNISHING

Once removed from the forms, the parts are put on pallets and sent to the "garnishing" department where they are assembled and aligned to match the original positioning of the Convent-approved model. An "M.I. Hummel" figurine may consist of as many as thirty-nine singly molded parts—as in "Adventure Bound" for example—which are hollow to prevent an explosion caused by the intense heat of the firing process. The hollowness and the production of the figurines in sections has enabled W. Goebel to achieve an elegancy and flow of movement that could never be duplicated if the figurine were poured as one piece. After the garnishing process, the assembled figurine is trimmed of excess ceramic material, dried, quality control checked, and marked with the Goebel registered trademark.

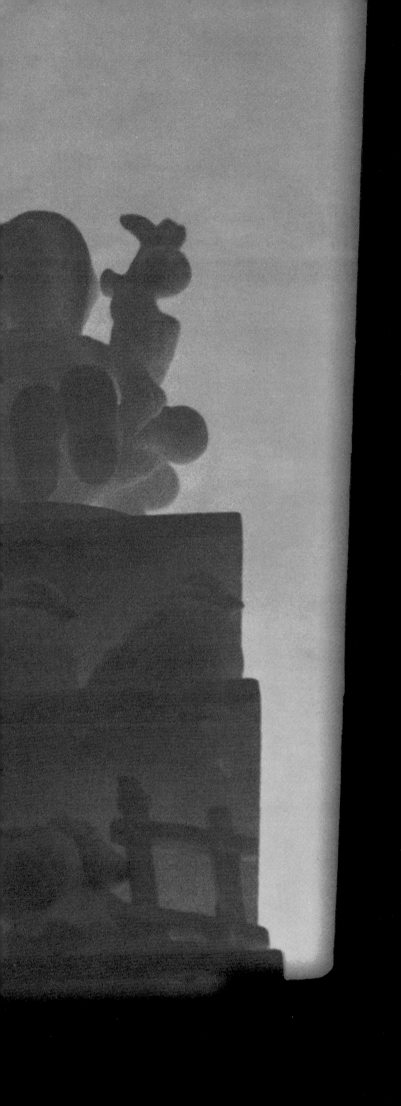

5 FIRING AND GLAZING

Placed on a car lined with refractory bricks, the figurine is then moved slowly through its initial kiln firing in the tunnel oven at a temperature of 2,100° fahrenheit. It is left to cool and then dipped or sprayed with a liquid glazing compound which colors it light blue. The blue color is merely an indicator to help the glazer ensure that the figurine has been totally covered by the glazing bath. The glaze, which is actually a liquified glass, gives a shine to the previously dull bisque figurines. The composition of the glaze allows the figurine to "breathe" during the second firing at 1,870° fahrenheit and combines with the hollow structure to keep it from exploding at the high temperatures. After a quality check, the figurine is put on a pallet and taken to the painting division.

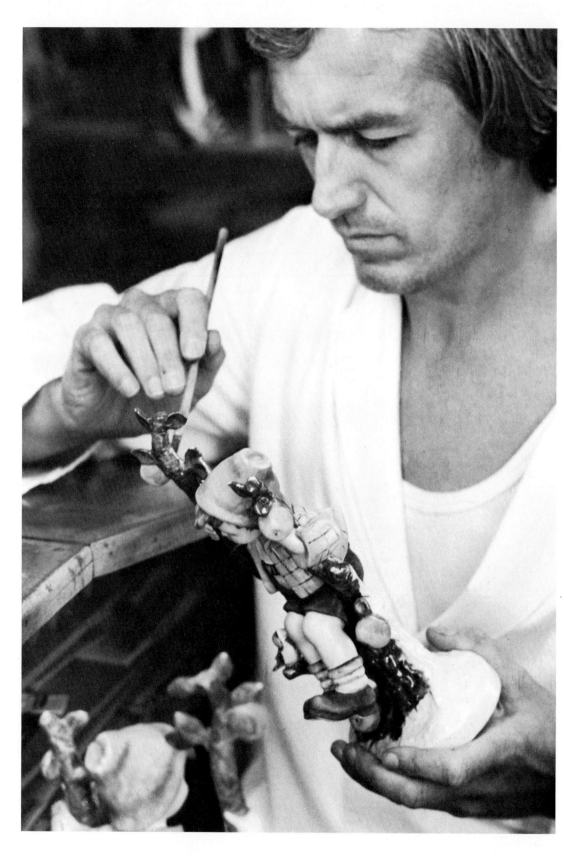

6 PAINTING

The painting of an "M.I. Hummel" figurine is a painstaking process. It is done by teams of artists who have undergone extensive training. In a systematic performance of thoroughly executed phases, the sharp eye of the painter coordinates the design of his figurine with the Convent-approved original. Over 2,000 color variations of ceramic paints are mixed daily for use on the various figurines in production, with master painters presiding over teams of about a dozen artists in bright airy ateliers. Paints are composed of metallic oxides and pulverized glaze with a small amount of oil base added. Iron, cadmium, copper, cobalt, chromium, vanadium, magnesium, and nickel are all used, and when combined with the glaze base and heated for the final firing at 1,407° fahrenheit, they melt into the figurine, giving it a matte finish once again.

From time to time the master painter will paint an initial or a number on the bottom of the figurine base to indicate that he and his team were responsible for the painting. Though this initial or number appears near the trademark, it in no way determines the date of manufacture or size of the model. It is a symbol intended for internal reference.

7 PACKAGING

After the "M.I. Hummel" figurines have been painted and fired for the final time, they are subjected to a last strenuous quality check—much more rigorous than those that take place when a figurine is passed from one department to another. Some figurines are sent back to the painting division for retouching, others are designated as seconds and destroyed. The majority of figurines go on to the packaging department where they are wrapped and placed in "styropor" boxes to eliminate breakage in transit. They are then inventoried and placed in large containers for direct shipment around the world.

TRAINING OF W. GOEBEL CRAFTSMEN

The legacy of porcelain and ceramic craftsmanship, passed from generation to generation since the days when it was a "cottage industry" prior to the industrial revolution, is a traditional form of artistry that requires not only talent but also patience for those who choose to learn. Nineteenth century Germany, recognizing the importance of specialized training for the porcelain and ceramic trades, was the first European nation to establish a technical academy, at the town of Bunzlau, to foster the art and ensure its perpetuation. A second academy was opened in the 1870s in the Bavarian city of Landshut. The profession of *Porzellaner* (porcelain craftsman) is not only a proud one but also a continuing one, with many German families encouraging their children to continue the trade. The W. Goebel *Porzellanfabrik* follows in this tradition by employing members of these talented families generation after generation.

Before beginning to manufacture "M.I. Hummel" figurines and other collector items, the Goebel firm established its own in-house school, which, in conjunction with the State Academy for Porcelain and Ceramic Arts in the town of Selb, continues to grant the diplomas for *Porzellaner* (porcelain craftsman) and *Porzellanmaler* (porcelain designer). In order to earn their diplomas, all Goebel candidates must complete a rigid three-

year course, a three-faceted program that combines factory training with classroom learning and three months of study each year at the State Academy in Selb.

Hiring by need, the W. Goebel firm strives to attract young students between the ages of seventeen and eighteen who have finished their high school education and are inclined toward the porcelain trade. Carefully screened for interest and ability, all applicants must pass a series of comprehensive examinations given by the firm. Only the highest scoring applicants are considered. Once accepted into the Goebel program, the future craftsman begins his three-year apprenticeship, dividing his time between the W. Goebel factory, the in-house classroom, and the State Academy at Selb. Students learn drawing, design, moldmaking, and the chemistry of porcelain and ceramics—not only discussing the subjects in theory but

also having the opportunity to broaden their knowledge through practical application as well. At the end of the three-year program, the student receives a diploma and is assigned to the particular branch of the factory for which he has demonstrated the greatest aptitude and talent.

With all the social benefits available at W. Goebel, work is a teamlike, almost familial experience. This spirit, combined with the outstanding leadership of the W. Goebel firm in the labor relations field, provides a nearly perfect working environment where craftsmen often spend thirty to forty years working at their trades, teaching and ensuring a younger generation that the great porcelain tradition of Bavaria and Thuringia will be carried on.

W. GOEBEL FIRM HISTORY
THE TRADITION OF THE COBURG-RÖDENTAL AREA

COBURG

KIPFENDORF

EINBERG

OESLAU

Inscriptions like this one denote the historic landmarks of the area.

The W. Goebel factory circa 1928.

The W. Goebel firm stems from a long tradition in porcelain and ceramics that began near the city of Coburg, Germany, over two centuries ago. During the mid-1750s, high-quality clay and sand were discovered in the village of Einberg, near Coburg, and in 1765 Johann Wolfgang Hammann founded the first porcelain factory in the state of Thuringia. Hammann's factory, in the town of Wallendorf, near the clay and sand deposits of Einberg, was known as the Wallendorf Works. Hammann's daughter, Christiana Catherina, married the artist Friedrich Christian Hutschenreuther of Wallendorf, and their granddaughter, Aline Hutschenreuther, married Franz-Detleff Goebel of nearby Reichmannsdorf.

In 1853, nearly twenty years before he was granted royal permission by the Dukes of Saxe-Coburg-Gotha to go into the porcelain business, Franz-Detleff Goebel applied to the local Coburg government for a permit to build a porcelain kiln. Answerable to the powerful Dukes of Saxe-Coburg-Gotha, the local government acted in fear of its royal leaders and informed Franz-Detleff that the construction of a porcelain kiln in Coburg would present a serious fire hazard.

Finally, on January 20, 1871, Franz-Detleff Goebel and his son William were granted permission to manufacture what was then known as Thuringer Ware, namely blackboards, slate, pencils, and children's shooting marbles. But Franz-Detleff would not stand to manufacture simply these goods. In 1879 he took his case directly to Duke Ernst II of Saxe-Coburg-Gotha to protest the delay. Shortly thereafter, in a surprising decision, Duke Ernst II gave his permission for Franz-Detleff Goebel to build a por-

On a nice day, W. Goebel workers often find it relaxing to take a leisurely lunch hour stroll.

celain kiln outside the city of Coburg in the village of Oeslau, only two miles from the rich clay and sand deposits at Einberg and Kipfendorf. In the same year, the F. & W. Goebel Porcelain Works began manufacturing their first kiln-fired products, items for daily use such as dinner services, milk pitchers, beer steins, and egg cups. Franz-Detleff Goebel had shown the local Coburg government what kind of wood he was hewn from.

At the turn of the century, after Franz-Detleff had died, his son William developed the firm's manufacture of porcelain dinnerware and figurines into an export-oriented business. Upon William's death in 1912, his son Max-Louis took over the business, and by 1914 the firm employed 400 workers.

A productive, innovative personality, Max-Louis Goebel influenced product design by inaugurating his own concepts and art forms. He surprised his customers with so many new porcelain figurine designs that he earned the name "novelty Goebel." His greatest innovation came in 1926 when he implemented the production of ceramic figurines to complement the porcelain line. Priced competitively, the ceramics sold increasingly well and other firms began to imitate his style. A decade later the breadth of this ceramic undertaking gave birth to "M.I. Hummel" figurines.

Max-Louis died in 1929. His son Franz assumed directorship of the firm along with his mother, Frieda, and his brother-in-law, Dr. Eugen Stocke. The trio, under the leadership of Franz Goebel, immediately began efforts to bring the firm out of the effects of the postwar economic depression and the resulting inflationary spiral. With the debut of "M.I. Hummel" figurines in 1935, the firm made a dramatic upsurge from the hard times that followed the First World War. But with the specter of Nazism hanging over Europe and the resulting wartime embargo of German goods, production slowed considerably. During the Second World War the firm concentrated on the manufacture of dinnerware for the domestic market, though some figurines were produced.

Just a few minutes from the factory, the renovated Schloss Neuhof (Neuhof Castle) is an example of traditional architecture. The Schloss now serves as a hotel/restaurant, with one of the largest private bird parks in Europe.

A stylized W. Goebel trademark in ornamental iron, adorns a factory portico.

Approaching a modern wing of the factory, one begins to feel the harmonious mix of tradition, old and new.

Summer colors brighten Coburg's traditional Saturday market.

Under the leadership of Franz Goebel, together with Dr. Eugen Stocke, the firm made a rapid recovery after the Second World War, largely because the U.S. Military Government of Germany quickly lifted the wartime embargo and gave permission for the production and exportation of "M.I. Hummel" figurines and other objects in 1946. U.S. occupation forces in Germany and European tourists comprised another important market for figurine sales, and by 1951—two years after the creation of the Federal Republic of Germany—the W. Goebel firm employed 700 workers.

By the late 1960s the great *Wirtschaftswunder* (economic miracle) of postwar West Germany had taken place, and W. Goebel, like many export-oriented German firms, had achieved great success. The firm was employing 1,400 craftsmen in the manufacture of "M.I. Hummel" figurines and other objects. Franz Goebel, who as a young man had lived in France, Canada, and the United States, continued to rely on his strong ability to judge the export market, leading his firm into an era of diversification and expansion.

In 1956 Goebel started a subsidiary in the United States. He also opened a toy and doll factory as a subsidiary in 1957, where the "M.I. Hummel" dolls are made. The *Oeslauer Porzellan Manufaktur,* later renamed *Oeslauer Manufaktur,*

Taking a break.

The Loreley, Coburg's oldest and most famous inn.

243

This stained glass window in the W. Goebel administrative wing celebrates the founding of the firm in 1871.

was founded in 1968 and produces high-quality porcelain dinnerware for both home and export markets. Shortly before his sixty-fifth birthday celebration in July 1969, Franz Goebel died. Franz Goebel's son, Wilhelm, and Ulrich Stocke, son of Dr. Eugen Stocke, took on the leadership of the firm with Dr. Stocke as mentor. This fifth generation took over the subsidiary enterprises as well.

Carrying on in the tradition established over one hundred years ago, Wilhelm Goebel and Ulrich Stocke have brought young and dynamic leadership to the Goebel concept. In the words of the current leadership, they are striving to achieve a second century "obligated to the past, dedicated to the present, open to the future."

The relationship among the directors, managers, craftsmen, and workmen is brought closer together through social and recreational activities. They have built a company sauna, a heated outdoor swimming pool, tennis courts, a library, and a day-care center for the young children of their employees. In keeping with this spirit, both the Goebel and Stocke families take an active interest in community cultural life and sports. Wilhelm Goebel and Ulrich Stocke make frequent visits to the production areas to discuss technical and job-related problems, and often take active parts in the factorywide employee meetings as well.

W. Goebel has continued to acquire new firms with great traditions of craftsmanship, thus sustaining the trend toward expansion established by Franz Goebel before his untimely death. In 1971, the Meudt Pottery Works was founded by W. Goebel for the manufacture of ceramic lamps and other items.

The ancient art of salt-glazed stoneware manufacture was kept alive in 1972 when W. Goebel acquired co-ownership in the Merkelbach *Manufaktur* of Höhr-Grenzhausen, near Cologne, whose blue and gray beer steins, mugs, and wine pitchers have been world renowned for over two centuries. In the same year they acquired the Charlottenhütte Glass and Crystal *Manufaktur* in Werdohl, where the difficult and ancient craft of hand blowing glass is still continued.

W. Goebel has become a modern, diversified firm by combining the creative planning of its leadership with the time honored skills of its craftsmen to win a place for its Bavarian and Thuringian handcrafted art objects on the market. The fact that "M.I. Hummel" figurines are sold in over eighty countries proves that the W. Goebel *Porzellanfabrik* and Sister Maria Innocentia Hummel's "Merry Wanderer" have taken a bit of Bavarian *gemütlichkeit* around the world.

The view atop the fortressed walls of Veste Coburg (Coburg Castle) glances down on the entire county.

Young children of W. Goebel employees spend their days playfully at the company's own kindergarten.

The long factory buildings run back from the main road for nearly half a mile.

CHAPTER 10: THE COLLECTOR'S PERSONAL JOURNAL

Here is an authorized listing of all "M. I. Hummel" figurines. Designed as a "check list," it affords collectors the opportunity to maintain a running account of all figurines acquired: where, when, and at what price.

HUM No.	NAME	SIZE(S)	WHERE PURCHASED	WHEN	PRICE PAID
1	**"Puppy Love"** *"Geigerlein" mit Hund*				
2	**"Little Fiddler"** *"Geigerlein" ohne Hund*				
3	**"Book Worm"** *"Der Bücherwurm"*				
4	**"Little Fiddler"** *"Geigerlein" ohne Hund*				
5	**"Strolling Along"** *"Wanderbub" mit Hund*				
6	**"Sensitive Hunter"** *"Jägerlein"*				
7	**"Merry Wanderer"** *"Wanderbub" ohne Hund*				
8	**"Book Worm"** *"Der Bücherwurm"*				
9	**"Begging his Share"** *"Gratulant"*				
10	**Flower Madonna** *Blumen-Madonna mit Kind*				
11	**Merry Wanderer** *Wanderbub ohne Hund*				
12	**Chimney Sweep** *"Ich bringe Glück," Kaminfeger*				
13	**Meditation** *Die Gratulantin*				
14/A&B	**Book Worm, Book Ends, Boy and Girl** *Der Bücherwurm, Buchstütze Junge und Mädchen*				
15	**Hear Ye, Hear Ye** *"Hört Ihr Leute," Nachtwächter*				

HUM No.	NAME	SIZE(S)	WHERE PURCHASED	WHEN	PRICE PAID
16	**Little Hiker** *Hans im Glück*				
17	**Congratulations** *Ich gratuliere*				
18	**Christ Child** *Stille Nacht, Jesuskind*				
20	**Prayer before Battle** *Der fromme Reitersmann*				
21	**Heavenly Angel** *Christkindlein kommt, Engel*				
22	**Holy Water Font, Sitting Angel** *Weihkessel, sitzender Engel*				
23	**Adoration** *Bei Mutter Maria, Marterl*				
24	**Lullaby** *Wiegenlied*				
25	**Angelic Sleep** *Stille Nacht*				
26	**Holy Water Font, Child Jesus** *Weihkessel*				
27	**Joyous News** *O, du fröliche*				
28	**Wayside Devotion** *Abendlied, Marterl*				
29	**Holy Water Font, Guardian Angel** *Weihkessel*				
30/A&B	**Ba-Bee Ring** *Hui, die Hummel, Wandring*				
31	**Advent Group with Candle** *Adventsgruppe mit Kerzen*				
32	**Little Gabriel** *O, du fröhliche . . . , Engel*				
33	**Ashtray, Joyful** *Gesangsprobe, Ascher*				
34	**Ashtray, Singing Lesson** *'s stimmt net, Ascher*				
35	**Holy Water Font, The Good Shepherd** *Der gute Hirte, Weihkessel*				
36	**Holy Water Font** *Weihkessel, sitzender Engel*				
37	**Herald Angels, Candlestick** *Adventsleuchter mit 3 Engeln*				
38	**Angel, Joyous News, with Lute, Candleholder** *Adventsengelchen mit Laute*				
39	**Angel, Joyous News, with Accordion, Candleholder** *Adventsengelchen mit Bandoneon*				
40	**Angel, Joyous News, with Trumpet** *Adventsengelchen mit Trompete*				
42	**Good Shepherd** *Der gute Hirte*				
43	**March Winds** *Lausbub*				
44/A	**Culprits, Table Lamp**				
44/B	**Out of Danger, Table Lamp**				

HUM No.	NAME	SIZE(S)	WHERE PURCHASED	WHEN	PRICE PAID
45	**Madonna with halo** *Madonna mit Heiligenschein*				
46	**Madonna without halo** *Madonna ohne Heiligenschein*				
47	**Goose Girl** *Gänseliesl*				
48	**Madonna Plaque** *Madonnenbild*				
49	**To Market** *Brüderlein und Schwesterlein*				
50	**Volunteers** *Soldatenspiel*				
51	**Village Boy** *Dorfbub*				
52	**Going to Grandma's** *Hausmütterchen*				
53	**Joyful** *Gesangsprobe*				
III/53	**Joyful, Box** *Gesangsprobe, Dose*				
54	**Silent Night** *Stille Nacht, Krippe*				
55	**Saint George** *Ritter Heilige Georg*				
56/A	**Culprits** *Apfeldieb, Junge*				
56/B	**Out of Danger** *In Sicherheit, Mädchen*				
57	**Chick Girl** *Kückenmütterchen*				
III/57	**Chick Girl, Box** *Kückenmütterchen, Dose*				
58	**Playmates** *Hasenvater*				
III/58	**Playmates, Box** *Hasenvater, Dose*				
59	**Skier** *Ski-heil*				
60/A	**Book Ends: Farm Boy** *Schweinhirt, Buchstützen*				
60/B	**Book Ends: Goose Girl** *Gänseliesl, Buchstützen*				
61/A	**Book Ends: Playmates** *Hasenvater, Buchstützen*				
61/B	**Book Ends: Chick Girl** *Kückenmütterchen, Buchstützen*				
62	**Happy Pastime, Ashtray** *Strickliesl, Ascher*				
63	**Singing Lesson** *'s stimmt net*				
III/63	**Singing Lesson, Box** *'s stimmt net, Dose*				
64	**Shepherd's Boy** *Schäferbub*				
65	**Farewell** *Auf Wiedersehen*				

HUM No.	NAME	SIZE(S)	WHERE PURCHASED	WHEN	PRICE PAID
66	**Farm Boy** *Schweinhirt*				
67	**Doll Mother** *Puppenmütterchen*				
68	**Lost Sheep** *Schäferbub*				
69	**Happy Pastime** *Strickliesl*				
III/69	**Happy Pastime, Box** *Strickliesl, Dose*				
70	**The Holy Child** *Jesulein*				
71	**Stormy Weather** *Unter einem Dach*				
72	**Spring Cheer** *Frühling ist's*				
73	**Little Helper** *Fleissiges Lieschen*				
74	**Little Gardener** *Die kleine Gärtnerin*				
75	**Holy Water Font, White Angel** *Weihkessel, Weisser Engel*				
76/A&B	**Book Ends, Doll Mother & Prayer before Battle**				
78	**Infant of Krumbad** *Jesuskind, liegend*				
79	**Globe Trotter** *Hinaus in die Ferne*				
80	**Little Scholar** *Erster Schulgang, Junge*				
81	**School Girl** *Erster Schulgang, Mädchen*				
82	**School Boy** *Schulschwänzer, Junge*				
83	**Angel Serenade** *Fromme Weisen*				
84	**Worship** *Am Wegesrand, Bildstöckl*				
85	**Serenade** *Ständchen, Junge mit Flöte*				
86	**Happiness** *Wanderlied, Mädchen*				
87	**For Father** *Fürs Vaterle, Rettichbub*				
88	**Heavenly Protection** *Schutzenengel*				
89	**Little Cellist** *Heimkehr, Bassgeiger*				
90/A&B	**Book Ends—Wayside Devotion & Adoration**				
91/A	**Holy Water Font, Angel looking left** *Weihkessel, Engel links schauend*				
91/B	**Holy Water Font, Angel looking right** *Weihkessel, Engel rechts schauend*				
92	**Merry Wanderer, Plaque** *Wanderbub, Bild*				

HUM No.	NAME	SIZE(S)	WHERE PURCHASED	WHEN	PRICE PAID
93	**Little Fiddler, Plaque** *Geigerlein, Bild*				
94	**Surprise** *Hänsel und Gretel*				
95	**Brother** *Dorfheld*				
96	**Little Shopper** *Gretel*				
97	**Trumpet Boy** *Der kleine Musikant*				
98	**Sister** *Der erste Einkauf*				
99	**Eventide** *Abendlied*				
100	**Shrine—Table Lamp** *Marterl—Lampenfuss mit Figur*				
101	**Table Lamp—To Market**				
102	**Table Lamp—Volunteers**				
103	**Table Lamp—Farewell**				
104	**Table Lamp—Wayside Devotion**				
106	**Merry Wanderer, Plaque**				
107	**Little Fiddler, Plaque**				
109	**Happy Traveller** *Hinaus in die Ferne*				
110	**Let's Sing** *Heini, Bandoneonspieler*				
III/110	**Let's Sing, Box** *Heini, Bandoneonspieler, Dose*				
111	**Wayside Harmony** *Vaters G'scheitester*				
112	**Just Resting** *Mutters Liebste*				
113	**Heavenly Song** *Stille Nacht, Adventsgruppe*				
114	**Let's Sing, Ashtray** *Heini, Ascher*				
115	**Advent Candlestick: Girl with nosegay** *Adventsleuchter: Mädchen mit Blumenstrauss*				
116	**Advent Candlestick: Girl with fir tree** *Adventsluechter: Mädchen mit Tannenbaum*				
117	**Advent Candlestick: Boy with horse** *Adventsleuchter: Junge mit Holzpferd*				
118	**Little Thrifty** *Spar-Hummelchen*				
119	**Postman** *Eilbote*				
120	**Joyful and Let's Sing (on wooden base)**				
121	**Wayside Harmony and Just Resting (on wooden base)**				

HUM No.	NAME	SIZE(S)	WHERE PURCHASED	WHEN	PRICE PAID
122	**Puppy Love, Serenade, and Happiness (on wooden base)**				
123	**Max and Moritz** *Max und Moritz*				
124	**Chef, Hello**				
125	**Vacation-Time, Plaque** *Ferienfreunde, Bild*				
126	**Retreat to Safety, Plaque** *Angsthase, Bild*				
127	**Doctor** *Puppendoktor*				
128	**Baker** *Der kleine Konditor*				
129	**Band Leader** *Herr Kappellmeister*				
130	**Duet** *Duett, Sängerpaar*				
131	**Street Singer** *Kammersänger*				
132	**Star Gazer** *Sterngucker*				
133	**Mother's Helper** *Mutters Stütze*				
134	**Plaque "Quartet"** *Bild "Das Quartett"*				
135	**Soloist** *Heldentenor*				
136	**Friends** *Gute Freunde*				
137	**Wall Plaque, Child in Bed** *Wandring, Kind im Bettchen*				
139	**Flitting Butterfly** *Sitzendes Kind mit Schmetterling, Wandring*				
140	**The mail is here, Plaque** *Trara—die Post ist da, Bild*				
141	**Apple Tree Girl** *Frühling, Mädchen im Baum*				
142	**Apple Tree Boy** *Herbst, Junge im Baum*				
143	**Boots** *Meister Wichtig*				
144	**Angelic Song** *Singendes Kind mit Engelein*				
145	**"Little Guardian"** *Betendes Kind mit Engelein*				
146	**Holy Water Font, Angel Duet** *Weihkessel, Engelgrüppchen*				
147	**Holy Water Font, Angel Shrine** *Weihkessel, Engel*				
150	**Happy Days** *Hausmusik, Kinderpaar*				
151	**Madonna** *Sitzende Madonna mit sitzendem Kind*				
152/A	**Umbrella Boy** *Geborgen, Junge*				

HUM No.	NAME	SIZE(S)	WHERE PURCHASED	WHEN	PRICE PAID
152/B	**Umbrella Girl** *Geborgen, Mädchen*				
153	**Auf Wiedersehen** *Auf Wiedersehen, Kinderpaar*				
154	**Waiter** *Herr Ober*				
163	**Whitsuntide** *Glockenturm mit Engeln*				
164	**Holy Water Font** *Am Wegesrand, Weihkessel*				
165	**Swaying Lullabye** *Kind mit Hängematte und Vögel, Wandring*				
166	**Ashtray, Boy with bird** *Ascher, Junge mit Vogel*				
167	**Holy Water Font** *Weihkessel, Sitzender Engel*				
168	**Standing Boy, Plaque** *Stehender Junge mit Herz und Flasche, Wandbild*				
169	**Bird Duet** *Frühlingslied*				
170	**Schoolboys** *Schweriges Problem*				
171	**Little Sweeper** *Kehrliesl*				
172	**Festival Harmony (Mandolin)** *Adventsengel mit Mandoline*				
173	**Festival Harmony (Flute)** *Adventsengel mit Flöte*				
174	**She loves me, she loves me not!** *Liebt mich, liebt mich nicht*				
175	**Mother's Darling** *Markt-Christel*				
176	**Happy Birthday** *Gratulanten*				
177	**Schoolgirls** *s' Meisterstück*				
178	**The Photographer** *Der Fotograf*				
179	**Coquettes** *Zaungäste*				
180	**Tuneful Good Night** *Wandschmuck in Herzform, sitzedes Kind mit Trompete*				
182	**Good Friends** *Mädchen mit Böckchen*				
183	**Forest Shrine** *Waldandacht, Marterl*				
184	**Latest News** *Das Allerneueste*				
185	**Accordion Boy** *Bandoneonspieler*				
186	**Sweet Music** *Zum Tanz, Bassgeiger*				
187	**M.I. Hummel Store Plaque (in English)**				
188	**Celestial Musician** *Himmlische Klange*				

HUM No.	NAME	SIZE(S)	WHERE PURCHASED	WHEN	PRICE PAID
192	**Candlelight** *Engel mit Kerze*				
193	**Angel Duet** *Stille Nacht, Engelgrüppchen*				
194	**Watchful Angel** *Schutzengel*				
195	**Barnyard Hero** *Angsthase*				
196	**Telling Her Secret** *Das Geheimnis*				
197	**Be Patient** *Entenmütterchen*				
198	**Home from Market** *Glückslauf, Junge mit Schweinchen im Korb*				
199	**Feeding Time** *Im Hühnerhof*				
200	**Little Goat Herder** *Ziegenbub*				
201	**Retreat to Safety** *In tausend Ängsten*				
203	**Signs of Spring** *Frühlingsidyll*				
204	**Weary Wanderer** *In Lauterbach hab i . . . ,*				
205	**M.I. Hummel Store Plaque (in German)**				
206	**Holy Water Font, Angel Cloud** *Weihkessel, Kind mit Blume*				
207	**Holy Water Font** *Weihkessel, Christkindlein kommt*				
208	**M.I. Hummel Store Plaque (in French)**				
209	**M.I. Hummel Store Plaque (in Swedish)**				
210	**M.I. Hummel Store Plaque (in English)**				
211	**M.I. Hummel Store Plaque with Merry Wanderer**				
213	**M.I. Hummel Store Plaque (in Spanish)**				
214	**Nativity set with wooden stable** *Krippensatz mit Holzstall*				
217	**Boy with Toothache** *Schmerz lass nach*				
218	**Birthday Serenade** *Geburtstagsständchen*				
220	**We Congratulate** *Pärchen*				
222	**Madonna Plaque**				
223	**Table Lamp, To Market**				
224	**Table Lamp, Wayside Harmony**				
225	**Table Lamp, Just Resting**				

HUM No.	NAME	SIZE(S)	WHERE PURCHASED	WHEN	PRICE PAID
226	**The mail is here** *Trara- die Post ist da*				
227	**Table Lamp, She loves me, she loves me not . . .**				
228	**Table Lamp, Good Friends**				
229	**Table Lamp, Apple Tree Girl**				
230	**Table Lamp, Apple Tree Boy**				
231	**Table Lamp, Birthday Serenade**				
232	**Table Lamp, Happy Days**				
234	**Table Lamp, Birthday Serenade**				
235	**Table Lamp, Happy Days**				
238/A	**Angel with lute** *Engel mit Laute*				
238/B	**Angel with accordion** *Engel mit Bandoneon*				
238/C	**Angel with trumpet** *Engel mit Trompete*				
239/A	**Girl with nosegay** *Mädchen mit Blumenstrauss*				
239/B	**Girl with doll** *Mädchen mit Puppe*				
239/C	**Boy with horse** *Junge mit Holzpferd*				
240	**Little Drummer** *Trommler*				
243	**Holy Water Font, Madonna and Child** *Weihkessel*				
246	**Holy Water Font, Holy Family** *Weihkessel, Heilige Familie*				
248	**Holy Water Font, Guardian Angel** *Weihkessel*				
250/A	**Goatherd, Book End** *Ziegenbub, Buchstütze*				
250/B	**Feeding Time, Book End** *Im Hühnerhof, Buchstütze*				
251/A	**She loves me, she loves me not!, Book End** *Liebt mich, liebt mich nicht, Buchstütze*				
251/B	**Good Friends, Book End** *Freunde, Buchstütze*				
252/A	**Apple Tree Boy, Book End** *Herbst, Junge im Baum, Buchstütze*				
252/B	**Apple Tree Girl, Book End** *Frühling, Mädchen im Baum, Buchstütze*				
255	**A stitch in time** *Zwei rechts-zwei links*				
256	**Knitting Lesson** *Ob's gelingt?*				
257	**For Mother** *Fürs Mütterchen*				

HUM No.	NAME	SIZE(S)	WHERE PURCHASED	WHEN	PRICE PAID
258	**Which Hand?** *Rat mal!*				
260	**Large nativity set with wooden stable** *Krippensatz, gross mit Holzstall*				
261	**Angelic Song** *Stille Nacht, ohne Kerzentülle*				
262	**Heavenly Lullabye**				
263	**Merry Wanderer, Wall Plaque**				
264	**Annual Plate, 1971, Heavenly Angel** *Jahresteller, 1971*				
265	**Annual Plate, 1972, Hear Ye, Hear Ye** *Jahresteller, 1972*				
266	**Annual Plate, 1973, Globetrotter** *Jahresteller, 1973*				
267	**Annual Plate, 1974, Goose Girl** *Jahresteller, 1974*				
268	**Annual Plate, 1975, Ride into Christmas** *Jahresteller, 1975*				
269	**Annual Plate, 1976, Apple Tree Girl** *Jahresteller, 1976*				
270	**Annual Plate, 1977, Apple Tree Boy**				
280	**Anniversary Plate, 1975, Stormy Weather**				
304	**The Artist** *Kunstmaler*				
305	**The Builder** *Der Schwerarbeiter*				
306	**Little Bookkeeper** *Stellvertretung*				
307	**Good Hunting!** *Weidmannsheil!*				
308	**Little Tailor** *Schneiderlein*				
311	**Kiss Me!** *Hab'mich lieb!*				
314	**Confidentially** *Zweigespräch*				
315	**Mountaineer** *I' hab's erreicht*				
317	**Not for you!** *Nix für dich!*				
319	**Doll Bath** *Puppenbad*				
321	**Wash Day** *Grosse Wäsche*				
322	**Little Pharmacist** *Der Apotheker*				
327	**The Run-a-way** *Der frohe Wanderer*				
328	**Carnival** *Fastnach*				
331	**Crossroads** *Am Scheideweg*				

HUM No.	NAME	SIZE(S)	WHERE PURCHASED	WHEN	PRICE PAID
332	**Soldier Boy** *Stillgestanden!*				
333	**Blessed Event** *Das grosse Ereignis*				
334	**Homeward Bound** *Heimkehr vom Felde*				
336	**Close Harmony** *Geburtstagsständchen*				
337	**Cinderella** *Aschenputtel*				
340	**Letter to Santa Claus** *Brief an Christkind*				
342	**Mischief Maker** *Der Störenfried*				
344	**Feathered Friends** *Schwanenteich*				
345	**A Fair Measure** *Der Kaufmann*				
346	**The Smart Little Sister** *Das kluge Schwesterlein*				
347	**Adventure Bound, The Seven Swabians** *Die Sieben Schwaben*				
348	**Ring Around the Rosie** *Ringelreihen*				
353	**Spring Dance** *Sommertanz*				
355	**Autumn Harvest** *Herbstegen*				
356	**Gay Adventure** *Frohes Wandern*				
357	**Guiding Angel** *Kniender Engel mit Lanterne*				
358	**Shining Light** *Kniender Engel mit Kerze*				
359	**Tuneful Angel** *Kniender Engel mit Horn*				
360/A	**Wall Vase, Boy and Girl** *Wandvase, Junge und Mädchen*				
360/B	**Wall Vase, Boy** *Wandvase, Junge*				
360/C	**Wall Vase, Girl** *Wandvase, Mädchen*				
361	**Favorite Pet** *Ostergruss*				
363	**Big Housecleaning** *Grossreinmachen*				
366	**Flying Angel** *Hängeengel*				
367	**Busy Student** *Musterschülerin*				
369	**Follow the Leader** *Mach mit*				
374	**Lost Stocking** *Hab mein Strumpf verloren*				
377	**Bashful!** *Vergissmeinnicht*				

HUM No.	NAME	SIZE(S)	WHERE PURCHASED	WHEN	PRICE PAID
378	**Easter Greetings!** *Ostergruss*				
381	**Flower Vendor** *Zum Blumenmarkt*				
382	**Visiting an Invalid** *Krankenbesuch*				
384	**Easter Time** *Osterfreunde*				
385	**Chicken-Licken!** *Kükenliesl*				
386	**On Secret Path** *Auf heimlichen wegen*				
388	**Candlestick, Little Band** *Leuchter Kindergruppe*				
388/M	**Candlestick on Music Box, Little Band** *Leuchter-Kindergruppe auf Musikdose*				
389	**Girl with sheet of music** *Mädchen mit Notenblatt*				
390	**Boy with accordion** *Junge mit Bandoneon*				
391	**Girl with trumpet** *Mädchen mit Trompete*				
392	**Group of Children** *Kindergruppe*				
392/M	**Group of Children on Music Box** *Kindergruppe mit Musikwerk*				
396	**Ride into Christmas** *Fahrt in die Weihnacht*				

CHAPTER
II: ANSWERING THE QUESTIONS MOST OFTEN ASKED

When was the first "M.I. Hummel" figurine made?

In 1935.

How many different "M.I. Hummel" figurines have been made thus far?

At present there are about 450 different three-dimensional "M.I. Hummel" motifs. The different sizes of a model are to be regarded as the same motif in this accounting. The 450 motifs include holy water fonts, madonnas, ashtrays, boxes, and lamps.

How old is the W. Goebel firm?

It was established in 1871.

How many people are currently employed by the W. Goebel firm?

Presently 1,500 persons.

Will there be more new "M.I. Hummel" figurines in the future, and how many?

Yes. Many new figurine models have been put on the market since the death of Sister Maria Innocentia Hummel in 1946. New models have been and will continue to be modeled by W. Goebel artists from the two-dimensional artwork created by Sister Maria Innocentia Hummel during her life as a religious at the Siessen Convent. Each model of a three-dimensional figurine designed by W. Goebel artists from the two-dimensional artwork of Sister M.I. Hummel is examined and approved by the Siessen Convent. Within the cloistered walls of Siessen, Sister Maria Innocentia Hummel sketched and painted, performing her mission as a Franciscan Sister, and in so doing, she created a great variety of motifs. Many of these have yet to be released as "M.I. Hummel" figurines.

Why does W. Goebel make so many other items and not more "M.I. Hummel" figurines?

W. Goebel is an expanding, diversified firm. The Goebel craftsmen who specialize in making "M.I. Hummel" figurines represent only a portion of the total work force. Therefore, the W. Goebel craftsmen who specialize in making "M.I. Hummel" figurines can produce only as many pieces as their handcraftmanship permits.

Has the factory ever burned down?

Never, though rumors persist.

Are visitors allowed and welcome at the W. Goebel factory in Rödental?

Visitors are always welcome at the factory. In fact, W. Goebel has built a contact center for this specific purpose. Visitors are also shown a film about the W. Goebel firm that includes portions about "M.I. Hummel" figurines.

Can visitors buy "M.I. Hummel" figurines at the factory?

Visitors to the W. Goebel contact center may buy up to three "M.I. Hummel" figurines at the German retail price.

Do all "M.I. Hummel" figurines have the name "M.I. Hummel" incised into the base of the figurine?

As far as production capabilities permit, W. Goebel incises its "M.I. Hummel" figurines with the "M.I. Hummel" signature. There are only a few "M.I. Hummel" figurines, which, for lack of space and technical reasons cannot be incised with the "M.I. Hummel" signature. These are the very small models of the collection.

Why do some figurines have little holes under arms or legs whereas other ones do not?

The firing process requires "air holes" on some models to avoid exploding figurines.

Where is W. Goebel located in West Germany?

In the northern part of Bavaria about seventy miles north of Nuremberg.

How many more Annual Plates are being designed?

Since the first Annual Plate was brought out in 1971, W. Goebel has put an "M.I. Hummel" Annual Plate with a different motif on the market every year.

What are the future designs of "M.I. Hummel" Annual Plates?

The motif for the next "M.I. Hummel" Annual Plate is made known about one year in advance of its introduction.

KERN COUNTY
LIBRARY SYSTEM